I love the tenderness, love, and encoura
book. *A Never-Give-Up Heart* would be a good read for *all* parents.

Karen McIntyre,
Bookstore manager, Rocky Mountain Calvary Chapel

The words in this book are a testimony of how God can provide grace to choose joy, show unconditional love, provide boundaries, and persevere through mountainous obstacles. I have been an eyewitness of how these principles have been lived out in the life of the author and her family. If *A Never-Give-Up Heart* blesses you only half as much as it blessed me, then you will be far better off for having read it!

Dave Stuart,
FamilyLife staff

Having taught children for many years who have challenges ranging from mild to severe, and having gotten to know the parents of these children, I know that the content of this book will address the needs of these parents' hearts and souls. The group study questions at the end of each chapter will give parents the opportunity to draw together and be encouraged as they seek God's guidance in their unique parenting situations. An outstanding book!

Peggy Jacobs,
EdD; Special Education Resource Teacher

My husband and I have watched Mike and Bev walk the road of "never give up," seeing the grace and strength given to them during the unexpected outcomes of life. *A Never-Give-Up Heart* is a resource filled with encouragement, helping parents recognize that this child who requires extra care and attention also has a very unique calling on his or her life.

Anne Marie Ezzo,
Growing Families International

As the special-needs coordinator at a large church, I know first-hand that when parents are faced with raising special children, fear can take hold. Beverly Linder has brought hope and tangible ways to help these families persevere and to see their situation through the Father's eyes. The principles in this book can touch the heart of any parent, and especially reaches out to a community of parents who can be isolated and discouraged.

Katie Garvert,
Special-Needs Coordinator, Woodmen Valley Chapel

A NEVER-GIVE-UP HEART

Raising Kids Who Face
Harder-Than-Average Challenges

BEVERLY LINDER

SH
Special Heart

A Special Heart Ministries, LLC

ISBN: 978-0-557-31809-4

Unless otherwise identified, all Scripture quotations in this publication are taken from the *New American Standard Bible* Copyright © 1960, 1962, 1963, 1968, 1971, 1972, 1973, 1975, 1977, 1995 by The Lockman Foundation. Used by permission.

Note to Reader: The ideas and suggestions contained in this book are not intended as a substitute for appropriate care of a licensed health care practitioner.

To Michael,
my love, my best friend,
and the best dad our children could ever have.

Note to the Reader

The scope of this book is very broad and includes issues ranging from mild learning challenges to severe disabilities—and everything in between.

Because of this, it is impossible to address each issue specifically, and it is probable that some of the particular suggestions in this book won't apply to every situation. Please look for principles even when the specifics don't exactly match your situation.

It is my prayer that the words of this book will in some way bring courage, hope, and perseverance to your hearts and homes. Thank you for allowing me to share my experiences and my heart with you.

Bev Linder

Contents

Acknowledgments   9
Foreword   11
Introduction   13

Part I

A Parent's Never-Give-Up Heart

Chapter 1   Never Give Up On Having Joy   21
Chapter 2   Never Give Up Showing Unconditional Love 29
Chapter 3   Never Give Up Providing Boundaries   43
Chapter 4   Never Give Up In Hard Times   57

Part II

Encouraging Your Child to Have a Never-Give-Up Heart

Chapter 5   Encouraging Character   69
Chapter 6   Encouraging Perseverance   81
Chapter 7   Encouraging Physical Health   103

Conclusion   123
Reflections of a Dad… by Mike Linder
Hope… by Brad Linder

Appendix A
You're Special (How to have a personal relationship with God)   129
Appendix B
How to Facilitate a Small Group   131
Notes   135

Acknowledgments

I am gratefully indebted to my husband Mike whose expertise and servant's heart helped to make a dream into a reality—thank you!

Many thanks to my dear friend Karen Stuart who always has a wise and heartening word—and who was such a great resource for children's literature for chapter 6.

Karen Leonard is a friend who is always there to cheer on, and has been that kind of friend to me in writing this book. What would I do without you, Karen?

To Sandi Eckert, forever the "prayer warrior"—thank you for being in touch with heaven on our behalf.

Bill Eckert offered time and support in practical ways when this book was only a seed of a thought. Thank you.

I'm thankful that Mark Wertheimer is a walking grammar-check! But more importantly, I'm grateful for the example he is of someone who truly loves kids.

Heart-felt thanks to Anne Marie Ezzo who encouraged me to employ a spirit of "coming alongside to help" in this book. I appreciate your wisdom and gentle spirit, Anne Marie.

To my neighbor Stella Soliz-Holmes, thanks for all the encouraging words. You make me feel like I have something worth saying.

Special thanks to Pat Reinheimer for imparting her valuable "know-how" to us.

Many thanks to Darla Hightower. It's so good to have a patient and knowledgeable friend who never tires of answering questions.

To our son, Ricky—thank you for being such a great sibling to your brother over the years—and a source of joy to your dad and me.

And to Brad, whose love of life and spirit of "never-give-up" has been the inspiration for all that is written here—thank you, dear son!

Foreword

Really it was Brad who taught us. As a student in our homeschool program at The Classical Academy, he schooled us in the real world. Starting out, other students may have seen him as different from them, but soon we all learned that Brad is Brad. As time went by, he proved to be an incredible example of perseverance and optimism in the face of daunting circumstances.

In *A Never-Give-Up Heart*, Beverly Linder encourages us to look at people differently—that people are souls, not bodies. She cites C.S. Lewis who said, "You don't have a soul, you *are* a soul. You have a body." Those who have different challenges can make us feel like an angel has visited us as they demonstrate that there is more to a human being than the outside.

We have all learned in tough circumstances to look for the "silver linings," but in this book we learn that the silver lining can define the glory cloud. These days it seems that life has become about avoiding suffering at all costs—to "a-muse" ourselves. Families who face the difficulties of dealing with special needs often find that their relationships can flourish as they go through hardship together. This is part of the glory cloud on the other side of pain.

The book shows us that God's style is to take things that look devastating and turn them around for the greater good. Take for example, the death of Jesus Christ on the cross. The greatest tragedy of all time became also the greatest victory. We see this in the scriptures, "And we know that all things work together for good to those who love God…" (Romans 8:28a) and "For our present troubles are small and won't last very long. Yet they produce for us a glory that vastly outweighs them and will last forever!" (2 Corinthians 4.17)

Ecclesiastes 9:10 says, "Whatever your hand finds to do, do it with all your might." May we all, including these very special kids, learn to find joy in doing whatever circumstances life may bring. That's the key.

Mark Wertheimer
Traut Core Knowledge School Principal
School Motto: Never Give Up!

Broken Dreams

When a child is born with a serious problem, or one becomes apparent, or comes into existence later, there is often a sense of grieving on the part of the parents—grieving over the dreams that they once had but that now seem impossible. My husband and I experienced this as well. It's a crushing feeling.

As the years have gone by, we have come to see that God has bigger dreams than what we originally imagined.

If our dreams revolve around having the best looking, the most talented, the smartest, the best performing, the most popular child—then we have a problem. But these are aspirations that God never intended for us to have. His desire always involves building a person who is strong on the inside. And our children have every bit the same potential as anyone else to develop character—perhaps more so due to the hardships that many of them often face.

Ephesians 2:10 says, " He creates each of us by Christ Jesus to join him in the work he does, the good work he has gotten ready for us to do..." (The Message). Do we suppose that our children who have limitations are excluded from this wonderful promise? I believe they are not excluded, and that there is a plan that God created for them, to touch the lives of others and to join with God in His ministry.

A PIECE OF OUR STORY

My husband Mike and I have been privileged to have three children. Our first child, Kristie Anne Linder, was born on May 25, 1986. When my husband saw her for the first time, he said that she looked like Cindy Lou Who, from the story of the Grinch—big eyes, sweet face, so innocent. But Kristie was born with a muscle problem, and to make a long story short, she left us to go to heaven when she was 3 years old. To give you an idea of our loss, I'll share with you the letter that I wrote her when she died:

Dear Kristie,

You have always been our special little girl. Even now I can hear you asking, "Mama, Daddy, am I your favorite girl?" Yes, you will always be our favorite girl.

You had three years of joy, and you gave us such joy. I can't remember a day that you were sad. You usually woke up singing, and nearly every morning you said, "This is a nice day, isn't it, Mama?"

No one ever knew you who didn't love you, Sweetheart. And I don't know of anyone you ever knew that you didn't love.

There are two things I most remember you saying. One is the phrase, "Some day I will…" Nearly daily you said, "Some day I will walk." "Some day I will dance." "Some day I will fly like Peter Pan." That some day is here, honey, and we are so happy for you.

The other thing I remember you saying is "Look at the clouds that God made." "Do you see the trees that God made?" It seems you were always looking up, always thinking about God. It seems that you were made for heaven, Sweetheart.

Oh Kristie-girl, we'll see you soon. How we look forward to that! We love you,

Mama and Daddy

Our son Ricky was born when Kristie was two years old, being healthy and happy. I'll share about him throughout the book.

Bradley was born in 1992, and we were crushed to discover that he had the same muscle disorder that Kristie had. When I think of Brad, I think of how some of God's best gifts come wrapped in plain, even torn paper. Little did we know at the time of his birth what a joy and inspiration he would be to us. I will be sharing more about him as well.

IT'S NOT THE END OF THE WORLD...OR IS IT?

When Kristie was born with a severe muscle problem, as a new mom I was confused and devastated. I remember another mom trying to comfort me whose son was born with Down syndrome years earlier. She said, "This is hard, but it's not the end of the world." Now, over 20 years later, I have remembered those words and asked myself, "Do I agree with what she said?"

My answer is both no and yes. I don't agree in that it really was the end of a certain kind of world—a world where everything is perfect and "normal." It was the end of that world, for having a child (and we have had two) with significant issues can bring the family into a situation where there are more doctor and therapy appointments than soccer games, and where money and time are often spent on hospital stays rather than family vacations. Yes, it was the end of a certain kind of world that we had dreamed of.

But there is another world, one that I would have never chosen, but that has proven to be a more fulfilling, meaningful, and in some ways, more wonderful, than any I would have ever imagined. It's a world where outward appearance becomes less important than the true person who lives inside, where unconditional commitment is given and received and a kind of love emerges that goes beyond natural love, where achievement is measured not by what others are doing but only by the uniqueness of the child in and of himself.

Although I don't like the hard things that our family has gone through, and I still often wish that our lives could be more "normal," I see the good that God has brought about in it all. And I wouldn't trade my life with anyone in the world.

ABOUT THE BOOK

Many of the moms who have attended *A Never-Give-Up Heart* workshop have commented that they can apply the principles I share to any and all of their children. In a way, that's the point. Raising a child with special challenges is in principle no different from raising any other child. However, the methods, the timing, the expectations, the amount of effort (blood, sweat, and tears!) are different from raising the typical child.

The purpose of this book is to touch on issues that are unique to us "special parents." We really do have a very different life than most of our friends who don't face the exceptional daily struggles that we and our children do. I've come to see it as a high calling, perhaps given to us because God felt we could do a good job with it. I hope that is the case. I know we really want to do a good job in raising these kids who have so much on the inside that is sometimes not noticed because of the external difficulties. Part of our job is to bring out the treasure that lies within so that God can use this child to bring blessing to others and glory to Himself. That's not just a sentimental thought—I really believe that this is God's design for our children—all of our children.

NEVER GIVE UP

Another purpose of the book is to encourage you to dream dreams for your child. A kind of strange thing happens when a baby is born with unexpected issues. Whereas parents are usually filled with hopes, dreams, and visions of what their newborn can become, we special parents often forego that privilege and begin asking the professionals what we can expect our child to accomplish and to be. While that has value to a point, resist allowing the perspective of any doctor, therapist, teacher, or well-meaning friend or relative to limit your hopes for your child—and especially don't allow anyone to limit your child's aspirations and goals for himself.

Only God knows "the plans" He has for this child, and they are good plans. "For I know the plans I have for you, declares the Lord, plans for welfare and not for calamity, to give you and future and a hope" (Jeremiah 29:11). No one can predict what the future holds for him. No one should assert that he "can't"—not when it comes to physical or cognitive skills, and especially not when it comes to developing outstanding character. There's a saying, "If you shoot at nothing, you'll hit it every time." Shoot at something. Aim far. You may not get as far as you would like, but it is certain that you will get further if you have some hopeful dreams. Your son or daughter deserves the chance to become all that he or she can be. Look beyond the limitations to what God might have in mind. And never give up!

PART I

A Parent's
Never-Give-Up Heart

Never Give Up On Having Joy

How does a person choose joy when there seems, at the time, nothing to be joyful about? This chapter will hopefully help to answer that question. In sharing a few details of my family's experiences with you, I'm hoping to bring phrases like "choose to have joy" out of the cliché realm and into the realm of real life—where circumstances can literally threaten to overtake us like a tidal wave but where there is a Rock where we can find refuge—and joy.

BUT LORD, I ASKED YOU FOR BREAD!

If you have not read the introduction of this book, please do—because it will give you an idea of the great loss we suffered when we lost our little girl Kristie when she was three years old.

Amazingly, I was somehow able to accept her death. Maybe it was because she was in a coma for so long and I was ready to release her into the hands of God by the end of those six weeks. My mother's heart just wanted her to be somewhere safe, and God gave me such a sense that she was really with Him, and ever so happy.

But my worst struggle came when our third child was born a few years later. You see, I had decided that what God was going to do was comfort us in the loss of our Kristie with a healthy baby girl. That was my first mistake—deciding for God what He must do!

On June 15, 1992 Bradley Caleb Linder was born. Not only was he not a girl, but he was born with a muscle condition even worse than Kristie's. And on top of it, he was a grouchy baby! Who wouldn't be—because of the odd position he assumed in the womb, his leg was broken during delivery. At first, all I could see were his problems, and as a result, I lost footing in my faith and crashed into depression.

I had been reading a book at this time entitled *Faith is Not a Feeling* by Ney Bailey. The theme of that book is truly life changing: *God's Word is truer than anything you feel; God Word is truer than any circumstance you have.*

During this time, I was in such an emotional storm that I prayed that God would rescue me before that storm completely overtook me. Suddenly, I got a crazy thought: *If only I could talk to Ney Bailey* (the author of the book). So I gathered my courage and somehow was able to get her phone number.

She was just rushing out the door to the airport but she took time to talk to me. I told her my story and she quoted me this passage from Matthew 7:9-11:

Or what man is there among you who, when his son asks for a loaf, will give him a stone? or if he asks for a fish, he will not give him a snake, will he? If you then, being evil, know how to give good gifts to your children, how much more will your Father who is in heaven give what is good to those who ask Him!

Ney shared this and then she said, "You probably feel like you asked God for bread and He gave you a stone—that you asked Him for something good and He gave you something bad."

Now even though I truly loved Bradley already and never saw him as something bad, I did see his condition as something bad. After all, we had just lost our daughter from complications from it—not to mention the sorrow we felt for Brad and the difficult life we knew he was facing. So I said, "That is exactly how I feel!"

Her response... "I can tell you that God has not given you something bad, but something good—because that is what His Word says, and God's Word is truer than anything you feel. God's Word is truer than any circumstance you have." And she prayed for our family as if she were storming the gates of heaven on our behalf.

"Before"

Through this conversation, God gave grace to believe His Word before I saw the truth of it. God's Word says we walk by faith and not by sight. He often calls us to believe Him before we can see what He is doing.

Ney Bailey encouraged me to believe God's Word and His goodness to our family *before* I saw it. During that time, a poem written by Amy Carmichael also came to my attention. It too encouraged me to trust God before I could see the positive parts of our situation:

> *Before the winds that blow do cease,*
> *Teach me to dwell within Thy calm;*
> *Before the pain has passed in peace,*
> *Give me, my God, to sing a psalm.*
> *Let me not lose the chance to prove*
> *The fullness of enabling love.*
> *O Love of God, do this for me:*
> *Maintain a constant victory.*[1]

And sure enough, it wasn't long before this baby with big problems began to blossom into a lovable, intriguing, and precious human being.

Oh, it hasn't been easy! Brad has had about 20 surgeries and lots of "close call" illnesses. Each of these times was heart-rending and stressful beyond what my husband and I sometimes thought we could endure, but it was all because we love Brad so very much.

A "Stone" or "Bread"?

So was this child that God gave us a "stone" or "bread"? Was he something bad or something good from God's hand?

To help answer that question, sharing a journal entry from a summer morning with Brad will give you a glimpse of what an encouragement and gift he is to me and to others as well.

Journal Entry:

This morning was one of those mornings that really happen about a zillion times, but today I felt it more. I was grieving over something going on in our family which made me "tearful." Brad is taking summer Band and the percussion section is at the top of some steep stairs. The good news is that the teacher said he wanted Brad up there rather than on the lower level because after just one class session he could tell that Brad could read music better than the others, and he wanted him up there as a support. The bad news is that I have to basically carry Brad up the stairs while his new peers stare at him. He is about to turn 13, and like all 13- year-olds, is very sensitive to peer opinion.

Anyway, when I returned an hour later, Brad was not playing his drums. I said to him in a rather threatening tone, "Why are you just sitting here when the others are playing?" A tear splashed down his cheek and he said that no one had handed him the paper he needed when the music was passed around.

When I got in the car, I, not Brad, fell apart. He said, "What's wrong? Why are you sad?" I said, "I'm sad because of a lot of things. But to be honest, I'm also sad that I have to carry you up the stairs and embarrass you in front of your friends. I'm sad because when you don't get a music sheet, you can't get up to get yourself one." I don't know if I've ever been that forthright with Brad but for some reason today, it seemed the thing to do. I guess I felt like he knew anyway.

Brad has been studying a book called, Boy, Have I Got Problems! *which is a youth Bible study on the book of James. He said to me, "Have you considered 'counting it pure joy'?" ...(James 1:2) I said, "No, actually, I haven't. Is that what you do, Brad?" He said that he tried to. Then he said, "Mom, what's a few steps and a piece of paper? That's nothing to lose joy over!"*

I knew that I had been visited by an angel. No one could have convinced me to "count it pure joy" at that moment except for Brad who was the one taking it on the chin.

We had a joyful rest of the morning together, shopping for Father's

Day and getting a birthday cake for Brad's party on Saturday. Every once in a while, I would look at him and he would break out in a big grin to encourage me. Thank you, Lord.

Yes, God gave our family "bread," something good—not something easy, nor something that has given us what is considered to be "the good life," but still, something good. I've come to realize that "hard" is not the same thing as "bad."

MESSED UP GOALS

When thinking of the biggest potential "joy robber" in my life, it has to be having my goals and plans messed up. What are some goals, plans, and hopes that have either gotten entirely messed up or have at least not turned out the way I expected?

The goal to have perfect health. Several years ago I got a horrible illness that I'm still dealing with to some degree.

As a newlywed, I had a goal to have a perfectly harmonious relationship with my husband. Although our relationship is good and I'm so grateful for this man, the goal of being perfectly harmonious will never happen!

I had a goal that our children would continually live in the values that we instilled in them with no intermissions or deviations. But, of course, this goal was unrealistic.

We have had a goal of financial freedom. But instead, we have had financial struggle.

I had a hope that I would never get wrinkled and old. That was kind of a dumb thing to hope for! Anyway, upon turning 50, I realized, forget about that one. Things are going downhill and will only get worse.

I could go on, but you get the idea! It's no wonder that we are so prone to lose our joy. So many of the things that mean so much to us just don't turn out the way we planned.

Now the above goals and the goals you have aren't necessarily bad. It's not wrong to dream dreams and go after good things in life. But there is only one goal in life that will never disappoint. *Nothing can ever happen that can keep me from doing the will of God, if I am willing.*

King David had this goal. In Psalm 119 verse 67 he says, "Before I was afflicted I went astray, but now I keep your Word." In verse 71 he says, "It is good for me that I was afflicted, that I may learn your statutes."

What is King David saying? He is communicating that the hard things in his life, the suffering and the disappointments and the hassles, have not messed up his life. No, because his goal was to do the will of God, he sees his trials as something to be grateful for. He's not grateful for the trial itself, but these things have driven him closer to his goal of keeping God's Word. This gave him joy.

There is a little sticky note on my bathroom mirror. It says:

Your will;
Your way;
Your timing.

Sometimes I can identify with the character Anne from *Anne of Green Gables* who was often, as she put it, "in the depths of despair." I too sometimes find myself in the depths of despair. But to the extent that I have maintained my joy, I attribute it in part to my little sticky note and to God's grace to submit to what it says—*Your will, Your way, Your timing.*

I would encourage you as well not to be afraid of yielding to the will of God. He desires our best. Isaiah 30:18 says,

Therefore the Lord longs to be gracious to you
And He waits on high to have compassion on you…
How blessed are all those who long for Him.

There's no need to be afraid of surrendering our lives to a God who feels that way about us. He is in control and He is good.

HAVING ETERNAL EYES

I don't know about you, but sometimes I ask God "Why can't things just be easier? Why do they have to be so hard? The answer to that in total will be a mystery until we get to heaven. But God has given us some answers in his Word. Let me share one with you:

In this you greatly rejoice, even though now for a little while, if necessary, you have been distressed by various trials, so that the proof of your faith, being more precious than gold which is perishable, even though tested by fire, may be found to result in praise and glory and honor at the revelation of Jesus Christ. (I Peter 1:6-7)

Did you know there is something we can do now that we won't be able to do in heaven? As far as I know, the angels in heaven have constant joy. They don't need to choose joy in spite of their difficult circumstances. But we have that opportunity! It glorifies God so much when His people choose to have joy—because joy is the evidence that there is more to this life than what we see with our eyes. Our joy gives evidence to the world that there is a personal God who lives within our very hearts.

I encourage you to take that circumstance in your life that seems like such a negative and to begin to see it as an opportunity. See it as an opportunity:
- to take God at His Word.
- to choose God's will as your primary goal in life
- to have an eternal perspective

As mentioned earlier, I had read a book entitled *Faith is Not a Feeling*. In a real sense, joy is not a feeling either. Joy is an attitude—a choice. And here's an amazing thing: Joy and sorrow can exist at the same time, in the same person. That may sound like a contradiction, but it isn't. In fact, the sorrow we carry around in our hearts gives the joy that we express to others a special dimension. It makes the joy more meaningful. And so I encourage you to never give up—on having joy.

Group Study and Discussion Questions

1. How can you apply this to your life right now: "God's Word is truer than anything I feel. God's Word is truer than any circumstance I have"?

2. Read Matthew 7:9-11. The summary of these verses is "If you ask God for something good, He will never give you something bad." How can you apply this truth to your life as a parent?

3. When have you seen God turn something into good that looked like something really bad at first?

4. What goals in your life have been "messed up," or have not turned out the way you had hoped?

5. Would it be difficult for you to pray the prayer "Your will; Your way; Your timing"? Why or why not? What kind of fears would keep you from praying this way?

6. Should you feel hypocritical or "fake" if you "choose joy" even when you don't feel joyful? Explain your answer.

Never Give Up Showing Unconditional Love

Unconditional love is the soil where children grow—in fact, it's the soil where we all grow. Without it we shrivel up and become insecure, bitter, and afraid to expand as a person for fear of being rejected or scorned if we do something less than perfect. I John 4:18 says, "There is no fear in love, but perfect love casts out fear." The context of this verse is not talking about parents and children; still I believe it is a principle about love that we can count on in any relationship. If kids feel secure in their parent's love, they will not be afraid to be who they are.

To show unconditional love to our kids is not the same thing as accepting all their behavior! It is not turning a blind eye and deaf ear to the areas where they need correction. Rather, it is helping them to understand that although their behavior, and sometimes their attitudes, need to be dealt with by a parent, they are always loved by that parent no matter what, and they will never be rejected as a person.

YOU'RE OK WITH ME!

Home is the place where the heart should hear often and in a variety of ways: "You're OK with me!" Then the bud will be in an environment to open to full bloom and the child's potential will be realized.

While sitting in church a few Sundays ago, I noticed in front of me a rather unkempt-looking teenage boy with his mom. Every once in a while, she would turn and look at him and give him a smile that said, "I like you just the way you are." I sat there and tried to learn from that mom. Wasn't she concerned that his hair was a mess and that he wasn't paying attention to the sermon? Maybe she was. But apparently even more important to her was that her son saw the look of approval coming from her eyes, which I'm convinced he did, and is probably why he was willing to sit in church at all. He'll grow up some day, and no one will remember what his hair looked like. But he will remember how his mom looked at him, and smiled at him.

Our special kids need to see that look of approval coming from us. We're only human, and we will fail in this at times. But some simple things we can do during the day will speak volumes to their heart: smile while making eye contact; give a little pat or hug for no particular reason; say something like, "I'm so glad you are my son/daughter." There is no question that these simple gestures coming from mom or dad will free the child to be a better learner, and make his spirit one that has a positive outlook and a fascination with being involved in his world.

I have come to realize that there's one gift I can give my child that surpasses any other human gift I may want to give—my acceptance of him. If a child feels he is a source of endless anxiety or an unwanted problem, he will be frozen when it comes to growing and realizing his potential.

Expressing this approval is difficult for any parent, but perhaps especially for us who have kids whose problems are so obvious and all-encompassing. But the benefits of getting into the habit of expressing approval toward this one who may rarely sense any genuine approval elsewhere, will be life-changing and God will surely honor our efforts.

FAMILY LOVE

All children need their "love tanks" filled. Perhaps the child who has greater needs and challenges even more so, for he is constantly faced with the question in his own mind, "am I OK?"

Ideally, the family should be the primary source of filling the love tank and of communicating both verbally and nonverbally, "you *are* OK."

The following thoughts are about sibling love, grandparent love, and parent love. Included are some excerpts and essays written by individuals who are qualified to share—because they have been great tank-fillers themselves.

Sibling Love

The sibling of a child with needs that are special can get tossed here and there. Some parents may favor the more needy child over the other siblings, trying to compensate for what seems to be an unfair shake for the child with the challenges. Other parents may be embarrassed of the child who seems so different and lavish too much attention on the other siblings or expect too much of them. Hopefully, in most families there is a healthy balance—but always the sibling of the special child has definite challenges in his or her life!

Siblings can be left in the literal or figurative waiting rooms of their family's attempts to make things go well for the special child. But has it ever occurred to you how important siblings are? Brothers and sisters will likely be involved in each other's lives longer than anyone!

It's crucial to encourage a positive relationship between all the siblings, and when it involves the child who has nontypical challenges, this can take some thought and discernment on the part of the parents.

The following five suggestions addressed to siblings of autistic kids can apply in principle to siblings of children with other kinds of issues as well. These tips were printed with permission from Autism Speaks. Other helpful information can be found at their web site: www.autismspeaks.org

Remember that you are not alone! Every family is confronted with life's challenges…and yes, autism is challenging…but, if you look closely, nearly everyone has something difficult to face in their families.

Be proud of your brother or sister. Learn to talk about autism and be open and comfortable describing the disorder to others. If you are comfortable with the topic…they will be comfortable too. If you are embarrassed by your brother of sister, your friends will sense this and

it will make it awkward for them. If you talk openly to your friends about autism, they will become comfortable.

While it is OK to be sad that you have a brother of sister affected by autism it doesn't help to be upset and angry for extended periods of time. Your anger doesn't change the situation; it only makes you unhappier. Remember your mom and dad may have those feelings too.

Spend time with your mom and dad alone. Doing things together as a family with or without your brother or sister strengthens your family bond. It's OK for you to want alone time. Having a family member with autism can often be very time consuming, and attention grabbing. You need to feel important too.

Find an activity you can do with your brother or sister. You will find it rewarding to connect with your brother or sister, even if it is just putting a simple puzzle together. No matter how impaired they may be, doing something together creates a closeness. They will look forward to these shared activities and greet you with a special smile.[1]

My son Ricky offers this advice from his own experience with his brother Brad:

I'm afraid that I never managed to determine very many methods of making my brother feel more a part of things while it really mattered, and I will forever wish I had. I was often at a loss, not because I didn't care, because I did and still do care. But I did do well in at least one thing and that is as Brad's older sibling I was often able to act as a social doorway to others and also just to be a friend to my brother myself.

Siblings of kids who have greater restrictions, and I think especially older siblings, have an incredible opportunity to be a stepping stone into the world outside of the family. A sibling can really help out by introducing his or her brother or sister to as many people as possible, showing the strengths of their sibling and showcasing a few ways to have fun together. After the initial example is made, young people are usually quite innovative in making up activities. Often all it takes is for the sibling to show others how it's done.

I also found it helpful to Brad to devote some time to his friends, even though they were younger than I was. I tried to make myself a part of my brother's life as much as I could, and I'm glad I did.

The Sibling Support Project offers a variety of resources for families of special kids and specifically for siblings. Following is a sample of what one sibling wrote:

I just want to tell all people, young and old, please resist the urge to stare at people who have disabilities. I do sometimes but after a while, I regret it. And don't take pity on my family! We are normal! Just because my brother has cerebral palsy doesn't mean we are aliens or anything! We have feelings, a brain, and a heart just like every other person in this world. So does my brother!

Written by Anne Mead, age 14 [2]

Also found at the Sibling Support web site is a section on "Siblings Who Have Made a Difference." This inspiring section tells of siblings such as the late actor John Ritter who because of his brother's cerebral palsy demonstrated his commitment and concern by being involved with telethons and fund raisers with UCP for many years. Another example is an adult sibling, Elena Villani, who is the primary caregiver for her brother Joe who has Down syndrome. She has an active career and is a volunteer at a hospice agency, yet makes sure that her brother lives a full and interesting life.

Yes, siblings are an important part of the special child's life. If you check out the Sibling Support web site, you'll see that there are significant struggles for siblings; this is normal. But in the end, there can be a great bond between siblings. Brothers and sisters can definitely be great tank-fillers for their siblings who have greater challenges than most.

Grandparent Love

When my daughter Kristie was born with an obvious problem, my parents came to visit us in the hospital. I remember posing a question to my dad through my tears, "Will you still love her?" His reply, "We'll love her even more." And that is just what he and my mother did with their first grandchild—they loved her as if she were an angel come down from heaven. What power there is in a grandparent's love!

The following is an article written by my husband's mom. In it she refers mostly to Brad, but she and "Grandpa Linder" also loved Kristie—just as they have loved all their grandchildren. In this article, which was originally a blog at http://specialheart.wordpress.com, Norma Linder shares some ways she has actively demonstrated a grandparent's love.

With grandchildren in four different states (none of which is my own state of residence) my opportunities to enjoy personal contact is infrequent. During my 23 years of being a grandparent each of these individuals has brought me joy, tears, laughter and pride in their various activities, decisions and accomplishments. One of them has faced from birth physical limitations that make every day a challenge that I have never faced on even one day. Thanks to the Lord for providing him with parents that have daily nurtured in him a spirit of positive attitude and perseverance. For example, as a seven year old he was tossing a basketball at a child sized goal from his wheel chair while I served as his "rebounder". After innumerable attempts to make a goal I assured him that he had done a good job of exercising his muscles and it was not necessary to sink a basket. But he was determined to achieve what he had set out to do and having learned from each attempt kept at his tossing until "Yes!" the ball sank through the elusive ring and netting. We both learned from that experience, especially me. I learned to give him all the time and effort that he was willing to spend to achieve a sense of pride and satisfaction in himself.

Each of these grandchildren has needs of one kind or another just as we all do. With a grandchild who has obvious limitations, some of the needs are more easily discernible. Grandparents should be aware of the power of physical touch. When sitting side by side, linking arms or holding hands is comforting to each participant. Somehow words are not needed. Laughing together over a joke, story or video can be a real bonding experience. If your grandchild is not verbal, laugh anyway. There may be inward laughing that we cannot observe. At any rate a joyful expression and attitude is desirable at all ages.

Make an effort to spend time with this younger generation and be open to listening without interruption This can take some discipline on our part. We older folks have so many experiences that we love to talk about. It is easy to miss out on hearing a special thought from these dear ones.

Most of all enjoy being a grandparent. Just as in parenting, the years with opportunities to develop a close relationship pass by all too swiftly, so enjoy each moment.

Parent Love

Our kids have a mirror that they look into each day to see who they are. It's our face. They look to see if they are an embarrassment or a source of parental pride; they look to see if they are a bother or a blessing; they look to see if they are considered to be capable in any way, or inadequate in every way; they look to see if they bring a smile of joy or a scowl of disapproval. It's scary, I know. Believe me I know how scary it is.

Karen and Jim Leonard are parents who know the value of reflecting a positive image in the "parent mirror." In the following blogs they share some specifics of how they have reflected that love to their son Steven, who has some audio processing issues. Karen starts with sharing about "missed opportunities."

There was an all too familiar story told a few years ago about an emotionally absent father and his son. The father loved his son, but was caught up in his high-powered career. The son longed to be with his father, and often asked if they could go fishing. The father finally said, "Yes", and they both put the date on the calendar. Oh, the son was beside himself! He had all his gear ready to go days before the event.

June 3rd finally arrived, and off they went. It was the day of days to the son. He treasured that time long after it was over. Years later, his father died. As the son was going through the father's belongings, he came across his dairy. He decided to look up June 3rd, the day that had meant so much to him. He couldn't wait to see what his father had written about the fun they had together. His father's entry read, "Somewhat of a wasted day, not much accomplished. Went fishing."

The first time I read that story, I was sad and furious at the same time. I know most of us are nowhere near where that misguided dad was. But, there is one lesson I glean from this story — missed opportunity.

I miss too many opportunities with my son. I get so busy doing things for my family that I forget to connect and delight in them. I struggle with (as most of us do), the balance between the demands of work, making healthy dinners, keeping our home cozy and pretty, relationships with extended family and friends and all the other things I can't think of at this moment, but are stacking up in my daily planner.

I have done a lot of counseling over the years, and there is one pain that clients have the hardest time overcoming. It is the sense or feeling that mom or dad didn't value them, like them, or want to be with them. Somehow, what mom and dad thought about them, deeply influenced how they saw themselves, how they related to others and how they were able to traverse life's joys and sorrows. Conversely, if a client had even one parent that demonstrated to them that they "hung the moon" so to speak, he or she often had enough of a base to face life's most daunting circumstances. This is an especially important point for kids who are different. Often, they do not have lots of friends validating that they are lovely, talented and important people. But, if mom and dad think they are gifted and delightful, they can soar above their difficult circumstances.

These thoughts have been powerful motivation to me. How do I demonstrate how much I value and enjoy my own son? Unfortunately, I still have too many days where we don't connect, where one of us is in a mood (we are both very emotional creatures). And, sometimes, it's just hard to get back on the horse and try again. But, when I do, and when he does, there is nothing better in this whole wide world!!

Here are some of the things we like to do together:

1. Eat popcorn and watch a movie of his choice.
2. Go to Starbucks and read books together. (I love coffee, he loves tea).
3. Jigsaw puzzles are recent favorites. Three hundred pieces is perfect for us; 1000 pieces makes my head spin.
4. Watch our favorite T.V. show—currently "Man verses Wild".
5. Weekly presentations. Each person takes 5-10 minutes to present something he or she found interesting during the week.
6. Have him teach me one of his computer games.
7. Go to any County Fair within 20 miles.
8. Look him in the eyes, whenever he is talking to me.
9. Touch him often—hugs, handshakes, high fives.
10. Go boogie boarding with him and his friends. There is something magical about riding a wave with someone you care about.
11. Draw. At this point, neither of us seems to have a "gift" in this area, but we do have some very funny looking "art".
12. Make movies on our computer (I Movie, for you Mac users)
13. Take an American Sign Language class together.
14. Cook together. He plans the meal; I am his helper.
15. Go fishing!

(You already know what my son will find in my diary)

Next, Jim Leonard tells of how some of his life experiences have contributed to his enjoying an unconditional love and appreciation for his son:

Sometimes the rear view mirror is clearer than the windshield. I look back on my high school days from this lofty height and see things I didn't then. I thought my purpose was learning math, English and Latin (yes, my school still taught Latin). Now I see my purpose was learning perspective and friendship. I sat beside a guy named Pat in one of my classes. Pat was not a great student. He spent hours on his work and rarely saw any grade higher than a D. I couldn't have cared *less. Pat was funny. He was an acute observer of people. His running commentary on the social tumble around us was tear-inducing. He spoke slowly and was often hard to understand, but it was worth the effort. I had a friend.*

I was shocked one day to overhear his mother and our English teacher talking in the classroom after school. Pat and I were just hanging out prior to heading home when, for no good reason, I stopped listening to Pat and picked up a matter-of-fact comment from his teacher to his mother about her son's "mental retardation." There were some guys who called Pat "retard" when they saw him, but they called a lot of people that. Suddenly Pat's bad grades and slow, slurred speech were not just peculiarities of my friend, but Symptoms. Pity raised its nasty head. Pat saw it in my eyes the instant it appeared. Our friendship changed.

A few years ago I was in a checkout line. My son, probably around 7 at that time, was waiting for me. Oblivious to the holiday press of people, Steven was acting out an imaginary story in a small but highly visible clearing nearby. As he gazed into another world, smiled, mouthed words, made gestures (with a sword? Wand? Ray blaster?), I watched with enjoyment. The lady behind me tapped me on the shoulder and asked, "Is he…?" She didn't finish her sentence. I grinned back. "Yeah, he is!" I said. I saw the pity in her eyes. I meant "amazing." I'm guessing she meant something negative.

We use all kinds of terms or labels for our kids. "Special needs kids", "Challenged", Different Learners". I prefer "Kids on the continuum". My own son has audio processing issues, but I can't understand why he, Pat, or any other child would be considered somehow "broken", because they don't fit into another's thought of typical or normal. God has made all children to be wonderfully creative and unique. They are within God's parameters, on the continuum. Our job is not to conform our kids to a standard of "normal," but rather to encourage them to bring their uniqueness to God's world.

I marvel at my son every day. My job is less to bend him to a social norm than to nurture what he brings to adulthood as unique gifts. With a lot of parents we know, their kids fit right into the middle of that bell-shaped curve. Hardly surprising – that's why that "bump" is there. With my kid, I'm heading in the direction of flattening out the bell-shaped curve, making it excitingly plumper at the edges, one kid at time. Maybe that's why I was attracted to friendship with Pat – God's preparation for my own future. So, here's to you, Pat. Your friendship was my training ground for perspective. And here's to all kids, every one of them on that wide and energizing continuum. May we help them thrive.

THE SOURCE OF PERSISTENT LOVE

Sometimes the stress of caring for the child with needs that seem so constant can take its toll on everyone in the family, and we may not feel very loving. But don't give up on choosing to demonstrate unconditional love. Feelings come and go; committed love can be unchanging.

What if we just can't conjure up this kind of constant and committed love? The source of unconditional love is described in I John 4:7, "Beloved let us love one another, for love is from God." When we stay close to God and seek Him daily, we can tap into the love that He has poured into the heart of every believer—"the love of God has been poured out within our hearts through the Holy Spirit who was given to us" (Romans 5:5).

The problem often comes when we head into our day equipped only with our own power, and our own power to love doesn't last very long. The following is a suggested prayer to pray when your feelings aren't cooperating with your heart desire to love your child unconditionally:

Lord, I'm having a hard time loving_____ . I'm tired and I don't even feel like trying. But your Word says that as a Christian the love of God has been poured out in my heart, and so by faith, I'm going to act lovingly toward my child and trust you to make my feelings follow my decision to love. Thank you that you love me—always, no matter what. I claim that this same kind of love is in my heart right now. In Jesus' name, Amen.

How blessed is the child who has family members who love him with unconditional love. This love will give a strength and resilience to face his world with confidence. I leave you with a poem from an unknown author who knew the value of never giving up on parent love:

To My Children

If you don't do well today
I shall love you anyway.
How you function—just your best
Is for you your only test.

How you struggle, how you try
Is what I will judge you by.
The world may consider just your goal,
I must look through to your soul.

I must see into your heart,
That I have borne and am a part.
As you struggle, I will pray
That you will win at work and play.

But if you don't do well today,
I shall love you anyway!!

—author unknown

CHAPTER TWO

Group Study and Discussion Questions

1. Read 1 John 4:18. Think about the comment, "If kids feel secure in their parent's love, they will not be afraid to be who they are." How have you seen this to be true with your child? What are some ways that parents can let their kids know that they are "OK"?

2. In what ways have you seen that family members such as siblings and grandparents can help the child with challenges to thrive and grow? What kinds of things would you like to see improve in these relationships?

3. How can a simple smile of approval on the face of a parent be a powerful source of motivation to a child?

4. Read what Karen Leonard wrote about "missed opportunities" in this chapter. Which of Karen's 15 suggestions sound like ones you would like to try? Have you tried any others that you would like to share about?

5. Read Jim Leonard's article "A Dad's Perspective on Loving His Son." What are your thoughts on his comment, "Our job is not to conform our kids to a standard of 'normal,' but rather to encourage them to bring their uniqueness to God's world."

6. Read I John 4:7 and Romans 5:5. Share some ways you can draw upon God's love in showing parent love to your child.

Never Give Up
on Providing Boundaries

Here are some questions to think about: Can you be a loving parent and still set boundaries for your kids? Do kids who have difficult challenges benefit from having discipline in their lives? Can kids who have ADHD and autism learn to possess a centered heart and self-control? How you answer these questions as a parent can literally determine the course that your son or daughter's life will take. Finding that wonderful balance between being tough and being tender as a parent is vitally important. It's often confusing for the parent of any child to know exactly where that balance is, but it becomes even more complicated when the child has additional issues to consider. This chapter will help you to explore these thoughts and hopefully gain some additional confidence in dealing with your special child.

DISCIPLINE AND LOVE

Discipline. It sounds ugly, unappealing, smothering. And it can be, if it is not the kind of discipline that God gives us and instructs us to give to our children.

Consider this passage from Hebrews chapter 12:

> *My son, do not reject the discipline of the Lord*
> *Or faint when you are reproved by Him*
> *For whom the Lord loves He disciplines…(verses 5-6)*

...whom the Lord loves He disciplines. That doesn't sound so ugly any more.

And what about us toward our children? Proverbs 19:18 says, "Discipline your son while there is still hope, and do not desire his death."

The wording of this proverb gives us pause—what does it mean? One thing is clear, that the writer of these thoughts felt that to discipline a child is to save him or her from harmful things in life.

This is God's kind of discipline—discipline that loves, and that protects.

I have noticed that often we parents of children who have harder-than-average challenges are hesitant to discipline them. After all, they already have a tough life, how could we dare to make it harder with discipline? Don't feel that way. It isn't true. To discipline your child is to love him—it is to protect him. Yes, we have to be aware that perhaps this child needs more nurturing, tenderness, or understanding than most. Maybe the results of the discipline will take a longer time and look different than some, but he still needs it.

Remember, "whom the Lord loves, He disciplines." And the same applies to a loving parent.

Part of discipline is communicating to our kids that we expect them to obey us. God's desire is to bless our children. Here is His command in Ephesians 6:1-3:

Children obey your parents in the Lord, for it is right. Honor your father and your mother (which is the first commandment with a promise) so that it may be well with you and you may live long on the earth.

Our children will advance faster and overall do better in life if they obey us, their parents. According to this verse, they may even live longer! Why? Because we love them and we want the best for them. This is why there is a promise of *blessing* for children who obey their parents.

PARENTING "TIMES"

Without a doubt, one of the most poetic portions of the Bible was written by the hand of King Solomon in the book of Ecclesiastes. Here's a portion of what he wrote in chapter 3:

> *There is an appointed time for everything*
> *And there is a time for every event under heaven*
> *A time to give birth and a time to die*
> *A time to plant and a time to uproot what is planted*
> *A time to kill and a time to heal*
> *A time to tear down and a time to build up*
> *A time to weep and a time to laugh*
> *A time to mourn and a time to dance... (See verses 1-8)*

There are also "times" in parenting. For example, there's a time to be firm and a time to be tender. Both of these can be motivational to kids in their own way.

Tough Love

It isn't harsh to be firm with kids. They need it. And perhaps they especially need it when they have unusually rough hurdles to overcome, because they often lack the confidence and courage to climb those walls of difficulty without a firm boost from their parents.

Last week I asked Brad to write a paper for home school. He has written papers before but this time it was to be with no help at all from me, and it was a multi-paragraph assignment. He is very good at some subjects, but struggles in areas where more subjective thinking is required. He knows he has this area of weakness, so after a time of wrestling with just the thought of it, he said, "I'm not going to write this paper." I knew it was fear of failure that motivated this declaration, so I said very firmly, "Oh yes you are!" He knew I meant it. He wasn't sure what consequence I had in mind, but he apparently didn't want to find out.

I could almost hear him "sweating bullets" as he labored over his work that afternoon. But when his dad came home, he read us his paper and it was better than we all expected. At bedtime he said, "I can't believe I wrote that paper!"

Anne Sullivan, Helen Keller's teacher, was not hesitant to be a little "tough" with young Helen. When she arrived at the Keller home for the first time, she instantly perceived this young blind and deaf girl's potential. She also recognized that Helen's opportunity for growth was being stifled with too much pity and overindulgence—so much so that she took Helen aside to a little cottage in order to be alone with her for some weeks.

Certainly Helen had much more significant obstacles than most to the learning process, but Anne realized that she was bright enough to overcome those obstacles. Before learning could begin, Helen had to get command of her impulses. Here are Helen's own words concerning her childhood days:

I was strong and active, indifferent to consequences. I knew my mind well enough and always had my own way, even if I had to fight tooth and nail for it.[1]

It's no wonder that Miss Sullivan felt compelled to be firm with Helen. She was at times the unfortunate recipient of Helen's antics. Following is a story that Helen recalls in her autobiography:

About this time I found out the use of a key. One morning I locked my mother up in the pantry, where she was obliged to remain three hours, as the servants were in a detached part of the house. She kept pounding on the door, while I sat outside on the porch steps and laughed with glee as I felt the jar of the pounding. This most naughty prank of mine convinced my parents that I must be taught as soon as possible. After my teacher, Miss Sullivan, came to me, I sought an early opportunity to lock her in her room. I went upstairs with something which my mother made me understand I was to give to Miss Sullivan; but no sooner had I given it to her than I slammed the door, locked it, and hid the key under the wardrobe in the hall. I could not be induced to tell where the key was. My father was obliged to get a ladder and take Miss Sullivan out through the window—much to my delight. Months after I produced the key.[2]

If you have seen the movie *The Miracle Worker,* you have gotten a feel for just how determined and uncompromising Anne Sullivan was with her student! But it was only so that she could have the incredible joy of teaching this young girl who was so full of life and potential. And teach her she did!

The application to us as parents? It is not a negative to be firm with our kids. Each child has different challenges, temperaments, and degrees of sensitivity. Therefore we can't simply take the experience of someone like Anne Sullivan and make it a model for how to treat every child who has a disability. But we can emulate Anne's resistance to think "she can't." We can take her example and approach the special child with anticipation that she can learn and grow, even in areas that seem to have such great weaknesses.

Tough love can give the child with supplemental needs a committed shove in the direction of growth and advancement. It really is one side of love—and there is another side as well—gentleness…

Try Some Tenderness

"Try some tenderness." Those are the only words in a song by Three Dog Night that I really remember from the lyrics that used to be popular back in my younger days. But they are three really great words, and they come to mind at times when I am dealing with members of my family.

In the last section, I talked about being firm with kids and that there was a "time" for that in parenting. But there is also a time for showing a gentle, tender spirit. Who can resist tenderness? Think of the last time someone was kind to you and the response that brought in return.

I remember once in particular when I was in a nasty mood, feeling like the whole world and everyone in it was a negative. I was in a grocery store at the time and I don't remember the details—only that right in the middle of my bad mood, a perfect stranger said some kind words to me. Suddenly, with just one person's gentle spirit, the world was to me a better place.

Our kids can get in nasty moods too; and kids who have daily struggles from their limitations really feel the heaviness of that load at times. That's the time to "try some tenderness," being that one person whose kindness can make the world seem like a better place to be.

Gentle tenderness does not come naturally to me. But I'm committed to make it part of who I am. We don't have to be resigned to live with our weaknesses. By God's power and grace, He can transform us "to the image of His Son" (Romans 8:29). He can make us a gentle person if we seek Him daily, asking Him to change us.

So, yes, be firm with your kids, especially in helping them gain self-control (because without it, it will be difficult for any parent or caregiver to be consistently gentle toward them), but all the while, sprinkle in a good portion of kindness—try some tenderness.

A CENTERED HEART

Remember *The Sound of Music*? At the beginning of the movie, Captain von Trapp summons his children to come with his whistle, to which they respond by marching down the stairs in unison. There they all stand in their drab sailor-like uniforms, standing at attention, responding not by name, but by a certain blow of the whistle. The kids are stifled, miserable, and cantankerous, especially toward nannies.

Then comes the new nanny, Maria, who wins their hearts, making them play clothes, teaching them to sing, and bringing out the best in their personalities.

Which is the role model for good parenting? Well, Maria, of course. No one wants to be rigid, stiff, and a killjoy! Right? Well, only half right, for here is a little-known secret: the teaching of self-control and of enjoying life are not in opposition to each other. They, in fact, go hand-in-hand.

Julia Child, the once famous and entertaining cook, said this: "You must have discipline to have fun." When I was a teacher, I would establish some very strict rules. Why? Because I wanted a stilted, regimented and boring classroom atmosphere? Not at all. It was because I wanted the kids to be able to have fun, and I wanted to have fun with them! I knew that there wouldn't be a lot of fun if I were constantly putting out behavior fires. But when the rules of the classroom were established, we could laugh, be creative, and really enjoy each other. And we did!

It's the same in a home and on an individual level. Self-control is the precursor to being able to enjoy life.

Some parents may wonder if their special child, whose challenges make self-control much more difficult than the typical child, is even capable of achieving self-management.

Norman Vincent Peale gave this great advice: "Make a true estimate of your ability, then raise it by 10 percent." That is also good parenting advice, particularly toward children who have difficult challenges. Yes, we are to be realistic about our kids' limitations, but we do well always to reach beyond the status quo, and better yet, to encourage them to reach beyond it for themselves. If we add our all-powerful and loving God to the equation, who answers prayer and desires to help us, we can expect improvement, perhaps even "far abundantly beyond all that we ask or think" (Ephesians 3:20).

Nature's Calming Effect on Kids With ADHD

Just about everyone knows that the incidence of ADHD has skyrocketed in recent years, especially in boys. Have you ever asked yourself why? Is it that it was previously undiagnosed? Is it stress level in modern kids? Is it parenting style?

Any or all of these factors may contribute to the situation, but allow me to share a contributing factor that isn't often discussed.

Richard Louv wrote *Last Child in the Woods*, which has the most interesting subtitle, *Saving Our Children from Nature-Deficit Disorder*. In it, he shares recent studies that have been done concerning the effect of natural surroundings on kids with ADHD. These studies indicate that kids with ADHD tend to calm down and function better in a natural setting. Even having a window to look out on "green" and beautiful surroundings helped many of them be more focused and centered. Here are his thoughts as to why young people did not seem to experience such hyperactive tendencies in the past:

> During…most of mankind's history, energetic boys were
> particularly prized for their strength, speed and agility…as recently
> as the 1950's, most families still had some kind of agricultural
> connection. Many of these children, girls as well as boys, would have

been directing their energy and physicality in constructive ways: doing farm chores, baling hay, splashing in the swimming hole, climbing trees, racing to the sandlot for a game of baseball. Their unregimented play would have been steeped in nature.[3]

My older son was home schooled most of his life so I can't tell you if he would be considered ADHD because we never pursued a diagnosis. I *can* tell you that during my pregnancy I often said, "I feel like there is a bucking bronco in my stomach!" And when Ricky was born, I discovered why. He was a constant charge of uninterrupted energy and nonstop activity. When he became school-aged, I asked myself, how does one educate such a child?

Lesson one: a large, open field and a butterfly net. I remember sitting on a towel and watching my son burrow through tall grass in pursuit of the yellow "flutter-bys," as he called them, experiencing the wonder of capturing them and putting them in an empty peanut butter jar for observation! We most often let them go, but "school" had happened in that meadow—and at least some of the "wiggles" had been released so that he was more ready to sit for a while and do traditional school when we got home.

Do what you are able to provide your child, especially if he or she tends to be hyperactive, with lots of play, chores, and just "hang-out" time outside. I know that in our society it is becoming increasingly difficult to find those opportunities to spend uninterrupted time in nature. When that is the case, don't completely give up on bringing nature opportunities to your home. Do things like having a year-round bird feeder outside the window of your child's study/sitting area, and planting trees close to the home where squirrels and other creatures can be observed from indoors; start an ant farm; have pets that you really notice. We once had two hermit crabs that would race on our kitchen floor from the center of a hula-hoop to the outer edge. There's something about such activities, even just watching, that releases tensions and brings a sense of calm in a child. No matter what manner of challenge your child faces, he will benefit from being in touch with God's creation.

Hyperactive and attention deficit kids do need boundaries, but they also need room to roam, and opportunity to enjoy the environment that God has provided for active little bodies to let off some steam. Give them that first, and then work on self-control issues. I think you will find your efforts much more successful.

What About the Autistic Child and Boundaries?

My answer is this: treat this child like a piece of fine china.

When I was very, very ill with an autoimmune condition several years ago due to a Candida overgrowth, there were symptoms that are amazingly similar to those experienced by many autistic children: severe food sensitivities and allergies, environmental sensitivities, intolerance of man-made fabrics, of florescent lights, and a hyper response to strong smells and loud sounds. As a result, I can somewhat relate to and definitely sympathize with the child who endures these disturbing sensations.

At the peak of my illness, God directed me to a kind doctor who said, "You are very fragile, like a piece of fine china or crystal. We need to treat you with this in mind." How relieved I felt that he saw me in this way rather than as a person with imaginary problems! Thankfully, since then, my hyper-responses have calmed.

Looking back at my experience, my doctor's words can be advice to parents of the autistic child: to treat him as a piece of fine china. Don't be afraid to parent and guide him with boundaries, accountability, and the kind of structure that all kids need. But do it all with an extra dose of care and gentleness.

Boundaries and Tantrums

Some kids are more prone than others to exhibit their frustrations in what is sometimes described as a "melt-down." These kids seem to have the unfortunate timing of expressing themselves in this way in public—you know, at the grocery store, during Sunday school, at the school's open house when all other parents are around.

Yes, I remember the feeling well—that desperate feeling of needing to say something to excuse my child's behavior—"He missed his nap." "He's getting over an ear infection." "He feels insecure in situations like this..." But somehow I felt no one ever believed me, or even cared about all my explanations.

Then in a parenting class we heard the "magic" words that got us through those tough days. Those words were: "I'm sorry. We're working on it."

That's all. No need for long explanations. Everyone has to work on things some times. And "things" that involve a child often take time and patient effort.

And then, really do "work on it." If you do, the day will come when you will see the fruit of your patient labor. Hang in there. Pray about it. Keep doing the right things, such as never rewarding the negative behavior in any way and never giving more attention to the child when he has a tantrum than when he behaves in positive ways.

I know it sometimes seems that as a parent you keep doing the right things and you see zero results. No matter how diligently you set out the boundaries, your child keeps returning to the same behavior patterns. I have a wonderful promise for you from Galatians 6:9: "Let us not lose heart in doing good, for in due time we will reap if we do not grow weary." In time, God will honor your efforts and both you and your child will enjoy the results.

TIPS FOR BRINGING CALM TO YOUR HOME

I'm sure there are a lot more, but these are some things that I have found to be most helpful in calming stressed kids:

- Music: Berthold Auerbach said, "Music washes away from the soul the dust of everyday life." Play music in the home. It doesn't necessarily always have to be "happy" music, but it should always be "good" music. What is good music? It could be defined as music that leaves the listener in a better state of mind and heart as a result of listening to it.

- Read to your kids: It doesn't matter if they understand all that is being read or not. Just sitting together on a couch and reading regularly can calm a child's spirit and make him feel valued.

- Massage: Touch your kids in gentle ways. A massage is a wonderful way to relax tired muscles and minds. Some kids don't seem to like to be touched. For these, just a light stroking of the hair might be good. Others may like a deep-muscle massage. Many autistic children are calmed by a certain kind of brush used on their skin. There's nothing more soothing than touch from someone who loves you.

- Avoid bright lights. You might be surprised how much lighting can affect moods. Use lamps instead of overhead lighting. Quality restaurants understand the effect of lighting. They dim the lights so that we will relax, hunker down, stay longer, and order more!

- Seek to have an orderly home. Your home doesn't have to be immaculate. But strike an atmosphere of order and routine. There's no question that kids tend to be calmer in an orderly environment where there is some structure and predictability.

- Alone time: Like grown-ups, young people need to be alone—to think, rest, and reflect. An established "room time" can be calming to the mind and spirit. This is not a time for electronic games; it is a time to build legos or play with dolls or look through books—or maybe just be still doing nothing but reflecting. If your kids aren't used to quiet, alone times, they may put up a fuss at first. But eventually they will be graced with the life-long gift of enjoying their own company!

CHAPTER THREE

Group Study and Discussion Questions

1. Read Hebrews 12:5-6. In what way is discipline a part of love (as opposed to the opposite of it)? How does this apply to us as we seek to love our children?

2. Why do you think that parents of kids who have needs that are special tend to be hesitant to discipline them?

3. Read Ecclesiastes 3:1-8. When you think of "times" in parenting, when is the time to be "tough" or firm, and when is the time to be tender?

4. Think of Julia Child's comment, "You must have discipline to have fun." How can a lack of discipline in a home make for an "un-fun" atmosphere?

5. Reflect on Richard Louv's observations on page 49 of this chapter. Do you agree that a lack of "nature time" and outdoor play can contribute to the symptoms of ADHD? Why or why not?

6. Review the section "Boundaries and Tantrums." Why is it futile to make excuses to others as to why your child is having a temper tantrum? Have you tried saying the words, "I'm sorry. We're working on it"? What kind of response have you gotten?

7. Read Ephesians 6:1-3. Why do you think that God included a promise to go with the command?

Never Give Up
In Hard Times

Our family has had its share of hard times, much of it involving our children. The apostle Peter warns us, "Do not be surprised at the fiery ordeal which comes upon you for your testing as though some strange thing were happening to you" (I Peter 4:12). I must admit, I am always taken back by the suffering that comes my way, especially when it involves my kids. Someone has said, "Life wouldn't be so hard if we didn't expect it to be so easy." We don't expect that a child would have to go through such difficult times, and we get confused. But the reason God, through Peter, reminds us not to be surprised is because suffering is part of life. Fortunately, for the Christian, nothing is haphazard. As Elisabeth Elliot has pointed out, "Suffering is never for nothing." I believe that, although often in the middle of the pain, it's hard to see the truth of it.

Allow me to share some things that God has taught me during those stormy times when I felt like I was going under, and I needed a life preserver to keep me afloat.

A PLACE TO HIDE IN HARD TIMES

Psalm 27 reveals that there is a "secret place" to hide in the Lord's "tent" during difficult times. "For in the day of trouble He will conceal me in His tabernacle; in the secret place of His tent will He hide me" (v.5). Perhaps the difficulty is as simple as having a bad day at school, or maybe it is more intense affliction that your child faces. There is no question that when our kids suffer, we suffer. But no matter the degree of pain, we and our loved ones may hide in this secret place and find comfort, rest, strength, and yes, perseverance.

Mike, Brad, and I just listened to a dramatization of *The Hiding Place* on CD. It is a true story of Corrie Ten Boom and her sister Betsy who were tortured and starved in a concentration camp for hiding Jewish people during Hitler's reign. When Betsy was finally breathing her last words in the filthy hospital bed where she died, she said to her sister, "There is no pit so deep that God's love is not deeper still. Tell everyone. They will believe us, because we have been here!"

Betsy had found that secret place, and the amazing thing is, it doesn't matter how hard things get, the hiding place remains a safe haven where joy and contentment can be found, no matter what. May we never face such a deep pit as Corrie and Betsy experienced, but in those hard times that do come our way, know that He is a refuge for those who seek Him.

ESCAPING FROM DEPRESSION AND "GIANT DESPAIR"

It's probably the English teacher coming out in me that I love old literature! I especially love an allegory written long ago entitled *The Pilgrim's Progress*. I remember a time when my son Brad was having a very rough time in the hospital. My older son Ricky and I were driving home late at night, in a blizzard, just to make things seem even more ominous. Ricky was eleven years old at the time and had been listening to a dramatization of *The Pilgrim's Progress* on his tape player. He loved it so much that he nearly had it memorized. I remember asking, "Ricky, how did Christian (the main character) escape from Giant Despair and from Doubting Castle?" He told me how Christian and his friend Hopeful had found a key called "Promise" and that key opened the giant's dungeon with ease. Then he said, "And by the way, Mom, the longer someone stays in Doubting Castle, the harder it is to get out!"

That "key" called Promise represents God's Word, His promises to us. I can testify that His Word has kept me from sinking into despair during times like losing our three-year-old daughter. It is His Word that has the power to give us eyes to see beyond our circumstances and enables us to believe that God is a good God with a good plan, in spite of what our feelings may be saying to us. God's Word has kept me from Giant Despair's grasp and made me strong when I was weak in myself. It hasn't always been without a great deal of struggle, but in the end, God's promises have held me up.

Kids need God's Word too. I bought a book in the hospital entitled *Praying the Psalms*. It paraphrases the Psalms in plain language in the form of prayers. I would read these to Brad as he lay in the hospital bed, playing soft music and sharing the truth of God's words to my hurting son. And I sensed that his spirit was also set free from despair by hearing the truth of God's love toward him. It helped to release his mind from fear and anxiety and reminded him that all is well, in spite of the difficulty of the situation. At the end of this chapter I have included some psalms that you can read to your child who may be hurting in some way.

GOD DESIRES TO BE CLOSE TO YOU

God wants you to know Him just as you know a close friend (see John 15:15). He wants to be your "Abba," which means *papa*, or *daddy* (see Romans 8:15; Galations 4:6). Jesus longs for you as a groom desires his bride (see Ephesians 5:25). Don't miss out on the practical benefits of drawing close to this God who so loves you! You never need to face hard times alone. And not only is He a close companion to those who seek Him, but He is the King of kings and the Lord of lords, and is able to come to your rescue and help those who are hurting in your family.

Following are some ways that I personally have found to experience that closeness to God that He offers. Perhaps some of these ways of seeking God will be helpful to you, or will at least stimulate some thoughts of your own as to how to draw close to your God.

Take a prayer walk. I love to take prayer walks every day. There is something about the fresh air and having no distractions that frees my heart to pray—and to listen to God. You can sing on your walk; or bring 3x5 cards to memorize Scripture, especially verses or passages that address your area of need at the moment.

Have a "date" with Jesus. Take your Bible to Starbucks. Let God speak to you through His Word. Perhaps record your thoughts in a journal, or write psalms or prayers. So nice to do this while sipping on your favorite hot drink! Don't feel self-conscious. Look around the coffee shop—you may find you're not the only one who is doing this!

Devote your first waking moments to God. I like to take a cup of tea and go sit in my rocking chair downstairs before I check my e-mail or do anything else. A friend once told me, "Go to the Throne before you go to the phone." It doesn't have to be a long time. For example, you can read a psalm out loud and offer a prayer of commitment for the day.

Take time to be with your God, your heavenly Father, your best friend, and the one who cherishes you as a bridegroom cherishes a bride. The hardest part of going through tough times is the feeling of being alone. You are not alone. Never give up on realizing His presence in your life, especially during hard times.

LIGHT SHINES BRIGHTEST AGAINST DARKNESS

Mike, Brad, Ricky and I once rented a motor home to travel from St. Louis to Colorado and then to San Diego. We found the RV to be a delightful experience, especially when we landed at a Grand Canyon campground for the night. When the sun set, because we were so far from any city lights, we saw an array of stars that left us with only one word in our vocabularies between the four of us—"Wow!" In the pitch dark they appeared immense in size and infinite in number. It was the blackness of the night that highlighted the brilliance of the lights above. Likewise, suffering can make a darkness in our lives; yet, in that darkness, God can often be seen as never before. All other sources of light that we depended on are removed, and He seems to make Himself known to us in a way that is out of the ordinary.

In spite of the night-time beauty of the Grand Canyon, we were glad the next morning when the sun shone again. In the same way, during times of suffering, we look forward to the brighter days. But don't forget to appreciate that glimpse of your heavenly Father that you get in the darkness, and encourage your child to look for Him there as well.

We can begin to think that because our lives seem more difficult than others' lives that our life is not as good. That just isn't true. We have sorrows that many others don't face because of the unique struggles of our children. Don't be afraid of sorrow. Don't think that your life is inferior because it may be harder, and sadder. Listen to this little piece of truth written by an unknown author:

"I walked a mile with Pleasure, she chatted all the way.
It left me none the wiser, for all she had to say.
I walked a mile with Sorrow and ne're a word said she,
But oh the things I learned from her, when Sorrow walked with me!"

PSALMS TO READ TO YOUR HURTING CHILD

(From *Praying the Psalms* by Elmer Towns, used by permission)[1]

These are just a few psalms that most kids can easily understand. If your child has a processing challenge and doesn't seem to understand, read them to him or her anyway. God's Word is "living and active" (Hebrews 4:12). I believe His Word can touch the heart of anyone who is exposed to it. Play some soft music, or if you are especially talented, put the words to a tune as you read.

PSALM 3

You, Lord, are my protecting shield
You lift me up with encouragement.
I cried out to You for help,
You answered me from Your holy mountain.

I was able to lie down and sleep,
Because You protected me during the night.
Now I am not afraid of ten thousand enemies
Because You are on every side to protect me. (verses 3-7)

PSALM 16

Lord, keep me safe;
Because I trust in You.
My soul said You are my Lord,
Apart from You I have nothing to hope for.

You have given me a good life,
I follow the good heritage of my godly parents;
I bless You, Lord, for guiding me throughout life,
You showed me what to do in dark times.
I have always made you my guide. (verses 1, 5-6)

PSALM 23

Lord, you are my shepherd,
I don't need anything.
You make me lie down in green pastures,
You lead me beside still waters.
You renew my spiritual energy,
You guide me in right paths;
To glorify Your name. (verses 1-3)

PSALM 27

Lord, You are my light and my salvation;
Whom shall I fear?

Lord, You are the strength of my life;
Why should I be afraid?

Lord, I will wait courageously for You because
I know You will deliver me;
I know You will come to me. (verses 1,14)

PSALM 121

I lift up my eyes to the hills,
But does my help come from there?
No! My help comes from You, Lord;
You made the heavens and the earth.

Lord, watch over me and keep me;
Stand at my right hand to protect me.
The sun will not harm me during the day,
Nor will the moon at night
Lord, deliver me from all evil
Watch over me as I come and go. (verses 1-2,5-8)

PSALM 103

As the heavens are high above the earth,
So great is Your love for us.
As far as the east is from the west,
You have removed our sin from us that far.
As a father takes care of his children,
So You love those who trust You.

All Your creation bless You, Lord;
Everything in Your kingdom
Joins my soul in blessing You, Lord. (verses 12-13; 22)

PSALM 8

O Lord, Your name is the most excellent one on earth;
You have glorified Yourself by creating Heaven.
You are praised by babies and infants.
But You will not accept praise by Your enemies.

When I look at the heavens, I see the work of Your fingers;
You planned the moon and the stars.
Then I realize mankind is so insignificant,
But You reveal Yourself to us who are just humans.

You made us lower than the angels,
And You crown us with glory and honor.
You gave us rule over Your creation,
You put it under our control.

You have given us sheep, oxen, and other animals;
This includes birds, fish, and sea creatures,
O Lord, You are our Lord;
How excellent is Your name on earth.

Elmer Towns, the author of these prayer-psalms, says this:

The very first word in the Book of Psalms is "happy", ashrey. This
book will make you happy when you pray its words and follow its
directions.[2]

Group Study and Discussion Questions

1. Read Psalm 27:5. This verse reveals that there is a "secret place" to hide in the Lord's "tent" during difficult times. Can you share a time when you have been there, protected by the Lord from life's storms?

2. John Bunyan, in his allegory *The Pilgrim's Progress*, shows the main character Christian caught in "Doubting Castle." What kinds of things in your life cause you to doubt? What doubts do you have concerning your child and parenting?

3. Reflect on the thought, "God desires to be close to you." Do you have a daily sense of His closeness? What kinds of things can you do to draw closer to Him?

4. Can you share some ways that you have been able to comfort a child of yours when he or she has been hurting?

5. Write a psalm or prayer to God about something that is going on in your life right now. Be prepared to read this to your group, if you would like to.

PART II

Encouraging Your Child To Have a Never-Give-Up Heart

Encouraging Character

What is character? I believe the answer to that question begins with what Jesus said in Matt. 22:37-39:

> *"You shall love the Lord your God with all your heart, and with all your soul, and with all your mind. This is the great and foremost commandment. The second is like it, You shall love your neighbor as yourself. On these two commandments depend the whole law and the prophets."*

With that, Jesus gave us the definition of character in a nutshell. It is to love God—having a "God-consciousness," that is, to care about what He thinks of our moment-by-moment decisions; and it is to love our neighbor—having "an aware-of-others heart"—being conscious of their feelings, their needs, their likes and dislikes.

When we talk about our kids having character, this is the foundation of what we are striving to develop in them. Character for character's sake can be self-focused, but true character always is God- and other-focused.

A GOD-CONSCIOUS HEART

Character in a child comes from his being aware that there is a personal God and that this God cares about the decisions he makes, both big and small. We all need something outside of ourselves to motivate us to consistently do the right thing. We can give our children external encouragement and even negative consequences to guide them toward being people of character, and that is a good start for young children, but ultimately they will need to have a sense of the reality that they answer to God in heaven. This brings about the kind of character that is operative "when no one is looking."

Our children, no matter what issues or limitations they may have, are made in the image of God. C.S. Lewis said, "You don't have a soul, you *are* a soul. You have a body." This is a profound truth for it tells us that there is a person within that body, even the body or mind that may be damaged or imperfect, that is made for his or her Creator. This child's spirit will only find true rest, comfort, and strength in a relationship with God, just as is true for all human beings.

Our challenge as parents is to know how to help our kids get in touch with God. Let me offer a couple of suggestions.

God has revealed Himself primarily in two ways on this earth—His creation (see Romans 1:20) and His Word.

God's Voice in Nature

There is a voice that is able to speak to and instruct any heart. It's a voice that speaks each day and each night, revealing a knowledge that transcends any learning style, bent, ability, or disability. Psalm 19 says:

> *The heavens are telling of the glory of God*
> *And their expanse is declaring the work of His hands*
> *Day to day pours forth speech*
> *And night to night reveals knowledge (verses 1-2)*

This "voice" is God's creation and is constantly "pouring forth" information about Himself and His ways. This never-ceasing flow of instruction is available each day for our enhancement and enjoyment, and is a teacher from God, able to touch any and every heart. No one is excluded.

You may have a child who seems incapable of learning about God due to a cognitive disability. Let me tell you about our family's friends, the Helds, whom we have known for almost 30 years. Their daughter Katie, who passed away a few years ago, had profound CP. This is what Sharon, Katie's mom, shared with me concerning giving input to children who seem unable to relate: "Give these kids a chance. Don't assume that they can't understand or take in simply because they have a difficult time giving out."

Give kids with physical, cognitive, or any other limitations the chance to experience nature. They may not be able to go hiking, but do things like letting them take their shoes off and wiggle their toes in the long summer grass. Bring them a dandelion to blow into the air. It's the simple things that can enrich the soul and teach the heart.

Here is what Helen Keller had to say about her experience with nature:

We read and studied out of doors, preferring the sunlit woods to the house. All my early lessons have in them the breath of the woods—the fine, resinous odour of pine needles, blended with the perfume of wild grapes. Seated in the gracious shade of a wild tulip tree, I learned to think that everything has a lesson and a suggestion. "The loveliness of things taught me all their use." Indeed, everything that could hum, or buzz, or sing, or bloom, had a part in my education—noisy-throated frogs, katydids and crickets held in my hand until, forgetting their embarrassment, they trilled their reedy note, little downy chickens and wild-flowers, the dogwood blossoms, meadow-violets and budding fruit trees. I felt the bursting cotton-bolls and fingered their soft fiber and fuzzy seeds; I felt the low soughing of the wind through the cornstalks, the silky rustling of the long leaves, and the indignant snort of my pony, as we caught him in the pasture and put the bit in his mouth—ah me! how well I remember the spicy, clovery smell of his breath! [1]

How wonderful it is that God's "voice" in nature is one that even the deaf can hear!

God's Voice in His Word

God's Word is the most perfect way He reveals Himself, and there are lots of ways to get God's Word into a child's mind. Just wander through your local Bible/book store and you'll find plenty of ideas. Allow me to share with you a few of our family's favorites that we have enjoyed over the years:

- Have a CD player by the bed. How great to have a child fall asleep to music or dramatic readings of Scripture. God's Word can touch the conscious and subconscious mind in this way. (You may want to avoid getting your kids "hooked" on having to have something playing in order to fall asleep. Use your discernment as to how often this is done)
- Get involved in a program like AWANA that has Scripture memory as part of it. Many kids who have learning disabilities are good at memorizing. Take advantage of that!
- Our family's personal favorite was to perform "dress up" night during a Bible lesson. We would all dress up in old clothes, scarves, headbands, and whatever else was around, and try to act out the Bible story we were studying. Learning God's truth in this way makes a lasting impression on young minds.

Whatever you choose to do, realize that your child needs that connection with God in order to become all that he can be. He needs internal motivation in order to have character take deep root in his heart and bear fruit.

I'll leave you with the most powerful thing you can do to nurture a consciousness of God in your kids. It is found in Deuteronomy 6:7 and it speaks of a parent bringing God into every aspect of life during ordinary, everyday times. Speaking of God's words, it instructs:

You shall teach them diligently to your sons and shall talk of them when you sit in your house and when you walk by the way and when you lie down and when you rise up.

When our own hearts and minds are filled with thoughts of God's ways, those thoughts will spill over onto our children in a natural way that does not need to be forced.

AN AWARE-OF-OTHERS HEART

Do you ever think of your special child as having a heart that is others-aware? With regard to a child with a disability, you may think of the goal as making sure that others are meeting *his* needs. And you should, to some extent. But to stop there is to rob that child of a God-given privilege of also being a blessing in the lives of others. The person who has challenges can show forth character in a wonderful way—in a way, in fact, that can greatly inspire others to do the same.

Even if your son or daughter has a condition that by definition makes it difficult to relate to others, don't assume that he or she can't demonstrate character.

Early in this school year, ten-year-old Kyle Forbes demonstrated an aware-of-others heart. Kyle is autistic to the point that others tend to make fun of him. But no one made fun of him when he demonstrated concern and bravery by saving his art teacher's life! They were both alone in the classroom before school started when Mrs. Lowe choked on the apple she was eating, blocking her airway. Kyle, who learned the Heimlich maneuver in cub scouts, saw his "next to favorite teacher in the whole world" in distress and ran over to save her life. It worked, and she likely wouldn't have made it if she were alone. His comment about the whole thing? "That was the first time I've ever saved someone's life!"[2]

Kyle's condition may cause him to be limited in relating to others, but it didn't stop him from being "others-aware."

Our job as parents is to continually nurture that spirit of being aware of the needs of others in our kids. Not often will the situation be as dramatic as Kyle's, but every day there are opportunities to guide our children toward looking beyond their own needs and desires to the needs and desires of those around them.

Respect Can Be Contagious
Respect is another form of being aware of others. To teach a child who has a disability to respect others is an especially high calling on the part of the

child—because often others may not show respect to him. Even if he is not overtly abused, he may be ignored, left out, and shunned. It takes living on a higher plane to show respect to people who have been insensitive and inconsiderate, or even downright mean.

This is how it was for my son Brad this past year. He was home schooled, but went into the local high school each day for band class. Many of the students at this school are, shall we say, a little "rough around the edges." One of the more bristly students showed up in the percussion section after being away for such a long time that we thought he was gone for good. (I think I heard him say that he got "kicked out" for a time.) Brad was not happy to see him because he felt he was just beginning to make some positive connections with his fellow drummers, and this student, Josh (not his real name), who was kind of a ring-leader, would ruin the improving atmosphere; Brad would feel left out again.

I suggested that he look Josh in the eye and give him a sincere and warm greeting whenever he had the opportunity to do so, which he did. I was in the room one of those times, and I heard Josh return a kind of grunt-like "hi."

One day, Brad told me that one of the drummers had helped him get his music sheets. (He often has trouble getting these because he is out of his walker and stuck in a chair.) I asked who helped him and he said, "Josh!" And can you imagine my husband's and my astonishment when it was Josh at the next concert who was making the effort to move things around to make sure that Brad was able to see the conductor? Recently Brad commented, "I think Josh likes having me around."

I'm not suggesting that showing respect and returning a blessing for an insult will solve all of our kids' social problems. It won't. But respect is often contagious, and if our kids learn to cast that bread upon the water, I believe they will see God's faithfulness to be true to his promise to bless their lives in return.

LITTLE THINGS

Yesterday I spoke with my twenty-one-year-old son Ricky who just got married last month. He was busy gathering addresses and anxious to send some thank you notes to relatives who had given him and his bride gifts for their wedding. This did my mother's heart good because I always made the often difficult effort of having my young kids send thank you notes to those who had given them gifts. When we do things like that as parents we wonder if any good in this world will ever come from it in the long run. I breathed a silent sigh of gratitude to God that these efforts were showing themselves in my son's adult life, and will hopefully translate into even more important issues of life.

Little things that we teach our kids make for big issues of character later on. Ronald Reagan said, "The character that takes command of crucial choices has already been determined by a thousand other choices made earlier in seemingly unimportant moments." As a mom who is coming to the end of parenting young children (what an irony it is that we finally begin to learn how to be a good parent when we are finished!) I encourage you to make those little efforts to turn your children's hearts outward. You may get a lot of complaining and resistance now, but you will often see the fruit of it later.

Here are a few suggestions to help develop that sense of otherness in children. The opportunities are endless, and you may already be in the process of turning your children's focus outward, but perhaps these ideas will spur some additional thoughts for you.

Pray with your children for the needs of others.

My friends Beth and Cliff are pray-ers par excellence! They have over the years, months, and individual days involved their four children in praying —heartfelt prayers, not primarily for themselves, but for others. Our family has been the recipient of some of these prayers, and our appreciation to have some devoted "prayer warriors" has been enormous during difficult times.

Do you suppose that their children have a soft heart toward others? You can bet they do. Prayer is probably the strongest way to turn our focus toward the needs of others. It doesn't have to be anything elaborate. This morning I suggested to my son, "Why don't you thank God for your breakfast and also pray for someone who you know could use some prayer." He did that gladly, and it wasn't a big deal in terms of time; but it was a big deal in terms of turning the focus of his heart outward at the beginning of his day.

Turn hardships into an opportunity for compassion.

Our family has been at the hospital a lot over the span of our son's life. Brad has been the one actually in the bed, but it's no fun for any of us, including the sibling who has to live through it all. For a number of years, on Christmas day, we turned our hardship into compassion by having our family take "goodie bags" to the people in the waiting rooms. We would start at the top of the hospital and travel all the way down, stopping at each floor to give out the Christmas cheer. I don't know if I have ever seen a room full of gloom change so quickly into a place of cheerful smiles! Brad in his wheelchair and the rest of us on foot, we would stop to wish each person a merry Christmas. Sometimes we would tell them that we knew how it felt to be in the hospital when we would rather be home. By sharing these Christmas goodie bags, Brad and Ricky got an idea of how the hard things in their lives could be turned around into something good for others.

The child who is aware of others is a happy child. You have a more difficult task in this than most parents, but don't give up. There will be joyful results if you stick with the challenge.

Expose them to role models who have an outward focus.

For many years, I attended the same church as Joni Eareckson Tada. Her life made an impression on me even though I don't think we ever spoke to each other (it was a big church!) Her eyes were always looking outward, focused on people. Her countenance was cheerful, evidence of someone who is not dwelling on her problems. She used her voice to sing to the congregation and her mind to constantly be thinking of how to encourage others in their struggles. And she still does that to this day, although now I live in a different state and don't ever see her in person.

I like my kids to be exposed to people like that, even if it is via the Internet or through books or movies. It gives a living picture of how someone can reach out to others in spite of—in fact, because of—his or her limitations.

Let your kids know that others are hurting too.

We used to do an interesting exercise in our home. Once in a while, we would eat only bread and water for one meal (no fancy bread such as cheese bread or bagels, and no butter!), and we would send the money we saved on that meal to someone who regularly didn't get enough to eat. This made the reason for sending the money more vivid to all of us as we wished we had more to eat! Depending on your child's condition, you may not be able to skip a meal, but consider encouraging your son or daughter to contribute some of his or her own money to sponsor a needy child. Make sure to show a picture of the child to make to make it more real. A young person's heart can become more sensitive to the needs of others through this kind of exposure.

IT TAKES TIME

There's something that we parents in our fast-paced society don't like about building character into our kids—it takes time. None of the suggestions above will yield immediate results. That is primarily because the human heart is not something that you can wave a wand over and presto! Human beings are complex creatures and because of this, touching the heart with convictions and passions and all the things that make for a morally excellent person takes years of nurturing, praying, and modeling. About two thousand years ago, a philosopher (who incidentally had a disability) named Epictetus said: "Nothing great is created suddenly, any more than a bunch of grapes or a fig. If you tell me you desire a fig, I answer you that there must be time. Let it first blossom, then bear fruit, then ripen."

Our efforts in guiding our kids toward being givers are well worth the blood, sweat, and tears that are required to do so. Jesus said, "It is more blessed to give than to receive" (see Acts 20:35). Since our Lord did not speak in sentiments, but rather in real truth to live by, we can assume that our kid's lives will be "blessed" if we point them in the direction of an other-focused life. We can also assume that young people who have limitations are not excluded from this life principle. They have much to give and people tend to notice it more when they do give. They have the potential to inspire. Because of this, persevere in guiding your child toward having a God-centered and aware-of-others heart. It will not only enrich his own life, but also the lives of those he touches.

CHAPTER FIVE

Group Study and Discussion Questions

1. Read Matthew 22:37-39. How are these verses related to developing the kind of character that is there "even when no one is watching"?

2. Why is it so important for our special child to realize that he or she is made in the image of God?

3. Have you seen that being out in nature has a good effect on your children? What are some ways to get kids outside even in our indoor culture?

4. There were several suggestions given in this chapter for getting God's Word into the hearts and minds of kids. Which ones of these would you like to try? Have you found any other ways that work well for your family?

5. Do you think it is more difficult for a child with significant challenges to have "an aware-of-others heart"? Why or why not.

6. Has there been a time in your life or your child's life when you saw the principle lived out that "respect can be contagious"?

7. There were some suggestions at the end of this chapter for helping our children to develop a heart that is aware of the needs of others. Can you think of any ways that you have encouraged your children to be others-aware?

Encouraging Perseverance

Fall seven times, stand up eight. So goes an old Japanese proverb. It is much like the proverb in the Bible that says, "A righteous man falls seven times and rises again" (Proverbs 24:16). The phrase "seven times" refers to many times or often (see Proverbs 26:16; Job 5:19).

If anyone needs daily and on-going perseverance, it is the young person who has a disability of any kind. Life is harder for this child. Things that come easily to others are often a major project for him. For those who are physically limited, simply getting from point A to point B can take stamina and energy that other children rarely need to put forth. For the student with a learning challenge, every new concept to learn can seem like a major mountain to climb. It's easy to want to give up. There is one character trait that will keep this child going day after difficult day—perseverance.

So before we leave the subject of encouraging character, let's take this one character trait and look deeper into what it means for special kids and how we can really help them to make it part of their lives.

THE GOAL: LESS SUPPORT

The child who needs more support than the typical child is in a tough situation, for being dependent on others is not something that the human soul likes. We all love the feeling of being independent. But reality is reality, and some kids need more support and are less able to be independent than others. For some it will always be this way; but for all, there can be a growing sense of independence, even if the progress is in small increments.

This quest for independence is a large part of what perseverance is all about for the child who has different challenges than others. Whether the independence is in the realm of physical, academic, or emotional areas, there needs to be a determined stick-to-itiveness in order to need less and less support from others.

We can kind of get "stuck" in our thinking in both small and in more important areas as it relates to our kids' growth in independence. To share a small example, recently I noticed I was hanging up my son's towel every time he left the bathroom. Then it occurred to me that when he used to have surgery after surgery, he was unable to do things like that—he was either in a body brace or his incisions hurt when he stretched forward. But now he is able! When I mentioned it to him, he said, "But you have always hung up my towel." We were both stuck! Then a few weeks later I took it a step further saying, "OK, I'll clean the tub and floor in your bathroom and you clean the sink and the part of the toilet that you can reach. Oh, and don't forget the mirror!" You know, I think he likes taking on this kind of responsibility. True, it's just a bathroom, but it symbolizes independence—not needing mom. And those areas of independence can continue to grow if we are constantly looking for new ways to back away from giving unnecessary support.

Scaffolding

When I was going through training as part of a language arts program for teachers, I learned of a concept called "scaffolding." The basic idea is that the teacher provides ample support throughout the learning process, at first, doing much to both assist the student as well as to model the desired learning task; then gradually, as the student gains more proficiency and confidence, the support is removed.

Things can get complicated for the special parent because when the typical child says, "I can't," we have more confidence to say, "you can." But when a child who has a disability or weakness says, "I can't," we are hesitant to push him for fear that we may be asking him to do the impossible, and we feel that wouldn't be fair.

As long as there is no anger or ridicule directed toward him if he fails, it is not unfair to ask the special child to reach beyond what he thinks he is able to do. Never stop evaluating and drawing the mark of the goal just a little further.

Think long term, for the day will almost certainly come when much of the loving support your child now receives will no longer be part of his adult world. It is the kind thing to do to be consistently weaning him or her away from needing any support that is not absolutely necessary. Here's an excerpt of an article that I recently read from a mom of an autistic young man who lives with her and her husband in his adult years, staying with them all day, every day. Here is what she said, "I'm 60. I'm not going to live forever. Who is going to care for him? Who will treat him with tolerance and patience? Who will love him?"[1]

I think all of we parents who have kids who require so much extra care look to the future and wonder what will happen. Humanly speaking, the only thing we can do to insure that our children will be able to function as adults in an adult world is to teach them the kind of perseverance that will daily bring them one step closer to the goal of not needing us. Obviously, most of our kids will always need some form of support that others don't. But we can get them as far as is possible. That is our part. The rest is in the hands of God, whom we can trust to care for our children even when we cannot.

I CAN DO THAT!

So what are some practical things we can do to encourage our kids to keep moving forward in this goal of becoming more and more self-reliant? There are two things that I often say to my son Brad that have helped us both to keep going during frustrating times: 1.) There is a difference between "I can't" and "It's hard." 2.) "Maybe you can't do that, but you *can* do this."

There's a Difference Between "I Can't" and "It's Hard"

Recently, I went into a store and left Brad to get out of the car into his walker by himself. It's no longer that he can't accomplish this, but it is still very difficult for him. As I shopped, I went back to the window of the store several times to see how it was going. At least two people went over to offer him help. But he said, "No thanks. I'm learning a skill." The people watching could barely endure seeing him struggle so. But they are looking at the short-term. In contrast, as his mom, I am looking to the day that he desires to live on his own, to go to college, to perhaps even some day get out of the car and escort a young lady on a date. These things may or may not happen, but he deserves the chance to try.

"Maybe You Can't Do That, But You Can *Do This"*

There are certain things that kids with special challenges can't do (yes, that's true for all kids, but not in the same way and to the same extent). So we persevere to help our kids do better with their weak areas. And there are some areas that just don't work at all. But the really exciting part of parenting the differently-abled child is to help him find what he *can* do! Because no matter what our child's limitations may be, there are some things that he is not only good at, but excels in!

That's how it was for Zach's mom, whose son was born with Down syndrome. She didn't accept that her son didn't have anything to offer, and she gave him the push he needed at each turn in life to prove not what he could not do, but what he *could* do.

The following is an excerpt from an article in CNNhealth.com:

> *"Sometimes you're scared as a parent, and you wonder if your child is going to be able to do this and this and this," Wincent said recently. "And you know what? You just go out and try it, and you live each day at a time, and you celebrate all the great things that happen."* [2]

Zach is now 19 years old. His genetic disorder, which causes intellectual disabilities and other difficulties, has not prevented "Zach Attack" from enrolling in community college, climbing the Great Wall of China, coaching hockey games or becoming Prom King at his high school.

Our children's abilities may lie in the area of arts, technical skills, intuition and kindness with others, and the list goes on. Most likely the reason that Zach was voted Prom King in high school is because he is an extremely likable person. Don't view skills like that as less important than academic skills. There's sometimes a trap that we parents get into— thinking that achievement in academics will totally equal life success. If you look at the past of many successful people, you'll see that just is not true. Academics can really help, but every person is multi-talented and it's a mistake to only look at one dimension. The same applies to physical skills or any other dimension in life.

Our kids may have disabilities in some areas, but they are *not* "disabled," for they also have areas of giftedness and *ability* (I believe, even in cases of extreme limitation). Be that little voice in your child's heart that says, "maybe I can't do that, but I *can* do this!" Help him see himself as a unique and valuable contributor to this world, because that is exactly what he is!

REBOUND! WHAT TO DO WITH FAILURE

My husband and I are studying a marriage book together. One of the sections talks about the importance of understanding the concept of "rebound," as in basketball. When the ball misses the hoop, it is simply an opportunity to get it and try to make another play. The principle is, when we don't do well in treating our spouse the way we should, to not see ourselves as failures, just as the basketball player doesn't stop and mope over his lack of success on the court, but rather to go for the rebound and try again.[3]

I explained this concept to my son as a life principle. Kids with special challenges have so many opportunities to try and to fail. It's important for them to understand that failure is just another opportunity to try again, to go for the rebound!

I'll share with you a little piece of a "rebound" story that happened at our house. Brad got the makings of a leather hobby for his birthday and just recently got it all out to make his grandpa a belt. For a couple of days I stayed and coached and helped. Then one day, after we had done some staining together, I said, "Brad, now that you know how to stain, I'm going to let you stain the remainder of the belt while I take a walk around the block. I'll be back in 15 minutes. (What could go wrong?!)

As I walked back in the door from my walk, Brad said, "Mom, you're not going to like what happened." With that kind of announcement, I kind of looked out of the corner of my eye at the table where he was working—the towel was drenched with stain as was the dining room table we have had for 28 years. I wish I could tell you that I was calm, cool, and collected in my response, but unfortunately, that would be a lie.

After we cleaned up (the table was fine for the stain was water-based), both Brad and I had the opportunity to "rebound." He got to try again at staining, and was successful. And I got to be the encouraging mom that I should have been from the beginning, even during the mishap.

If we hadn't gone for the rebound, we would have both left that situation feeling like failures. Brad probably would never have wanted to try his new hobby again, and I would have felt like a terrible mom. But we both got to try again.

What could be more freeing than to know that mistakes, failures, and even sins (because of our forgiveness in Christ) don't have to bring us down? We don't have to evaluate our lives based on our failures, and neither do our kids. This all takes grace toward one another and toward ourselves to know that there is a new, fresh start each moment. God extends this grace to us, and we should be free to give it to ourselves and to our kids, teaching them to take that fresh start and to put the failure behind them—in all areas of life. Avoid any communication that includes thoughts such as "all is lost," "the damage is done," "it's no use," "it'll never happen."

Did your child have a meltdown in class? Encourage him to go back and show self-control and courtesy to his classmates. Was he unable to participate in something he would like to be a part of because of a physical limitation? Help him to think of new ways of trying or to simply be able to enjoy watching others enjoy themselves and to cheer them on. Did she fail yet another school assignment? Help her to rebound and to approach the challenge from a way that will help her to be successful next time. Or get her in a different situation where failure isn't so likely, such as, for example, home schooling.

And how about you? Have you failed at being an encouraging parent? Rebound, start fresh. Do better today. Our Lord's "mercies are new every morning" (Lamentations 3: 22-23).

The ability to start again after failing in any dimension of life, whether it is in relationships, skills, or life endeavors is really at the foundation of having a heart of perseverance.

POSITIVE OUTLOOK, THE STRENGTH BEHIND PERSEVERANCE

We all have "Eeyore" days and moments when nothing can convince us that there is anything good in our lives. The child who has a disability is not imagining his plight, for each day is filled with abundant challenges that most others never have to face. There is indeed good reason to feel gloomy when life is so difficult. Still, because we love our child, we must encourage him to turn his focus away from his problems. If we don't, he may get into a life habit that will make him prone toward misery and will destroy his potential to be involved in the lives of others in a positive way.

I often feel hesitant to ask my son to look at the positive side of life, knowing how badly I would struggle if I were "in his shoes," dealing with what he has to deal with on a daily basis. But God's Word tells me that he has grace that is abundant and that shows itself more powerfully in weakness. "My grace is sufficient for you, for power is perfected in weakness" (2 Corinthians 12:9). God also comforts "the depressed" and those who are "afflicted" (2 Corinthians 1:3-4; 2 Corinthians 7:6). Knowing that God gives grace to those who are weak, and who tend to be depressed and afflicted, makes me able to encourage my son to lay hold of that grace and to find the joy that each day has to offer, in spite of the difficulties.

This week I have been reading Hebrews chapter 12. Verse 2 says that we should "fix our eyes on Jesus" in running the "race" of the Christian life. God is encouraging us to learn to focus. Where we look with the eyes of our hearts is where our emotions and thoughts will carry us.

There are things we can do to help a child who is down turn his focus toward the positive things in life. The following are some suggestions.

1. Play cheerful, quality music.
2. Read to him inspirational stories, both true and fiction.
3. Watch movies that inspire one to live beyond the circumstances. (See the end of this chapter for ideas on books and movies that can inspire kids to persevere.)
4. Point out daily blessings in conversation, not making a big deal of it, simply mentioning the positive things that life brings.
5. Make his day filled with variety and positive challenges.
6. Tell him he is a blessing to you.
7. Pray with and for your child. Pray for him in his presence. Thank God for him and be specific. Encourage him to pray out loud—prayers of thanksgiving.
8. Get him outside!
9. Read God's promises to him—or have him read them himself, if possible.
10. Smile at him or her–a lot!!

Take special note of that last point. Smile at your beloved child. It just might be contagious; and if he sees that look of delight in your eyes toward him consistently, he will come to believe that he is worth smiling about! There will be power there to lift him out of the slumps of life.

BUT I'M SO TIRED!

You may be reading this chapter and really wanting to have and to nurture that spirit of "keepin' on" but you are just plain tired from the day-in-and-day-out struggles of life.

I hope that my encouragement to persevere doesn't sound like empty cheerleading or like someone who doesn't understand the strain you are under. I sometimes just want to cry from the strain (and sometimes do!) and I know that my loved ones feel that way too.

When things seem overwhelming, give up the attempts for that day. Find a quiet place to read and to meditate on what is true, relax in whatever way is helpful to you (for me, there's nothing like a hot bath), get a good night's sleep and begin again the next day. Give your mind and soul a rest whenever you need it, and give that to your child when he or she needs it as well. Take whatever time you need to refresh yourselves and begin again when you sense that you and your child are ready.

When pressures seem to be crushing on you and your family, stop everything, give your loved ones a hug, and just enjoy each other for a while. Stop your labors and give yourself and everyone involved not only a break, but also some loving attention that is not focused on solving any life problem. Bake some cookies; do a jigsaw puzzle; read in the same room quietly— anything to lighten up for a while.

Physical, mental, and emotional rest are essential to this process of persevering. And there is also a spiritual rest that, if we grasp it, can give us a calm spirit even in the midst of the pressures of life. Psalm 127 gives us some insight into God's part in this process of persevering:

> *Unless the Lord builds the house,*
> *They labor in vain who build it*
> *Unless the Lord guards the city*
> *The watchman keeps awake in vain*
> *It is vain for you to rise up early*
> *To retire late*
> *To eat the bread of painful labors*
> *For he gives to His beloved*
> *Even in his sleep. (verses 1-2)*

Helping our kids is just plain hard work! But the results are from the Lord. Sometimes, when I feel helpless, I stop and lay my hand on my son and pray for him silently, acknowledging that only God can really accomplish what needs to be accomplished. Notice in the psalm, that God can touch our children even while we are all asleep! Also notice that it is "vain" or useless to strive to the point of exhaustion. Keith Green wrote a song that said, "Just keep doing your best, and pray that it's blessed, and He'll take care of the rest!"

Perseverance and rest go hand in hand. One without the other will not accomplish what needs to be done for our kids. And when it comes to resting in the Lord, that is a 24/7 privilege, for His rest is available even at the very time that we work so hard toward our goals. Our bodies and minds may be persevering, but our souls can be at rest.

THE POWER OF GOOD LITERATURE

"I will take it. I will take the ring to Mordor…though I do not know the way." (the determination and character of Frodo Baggins, *The Lord of the Rings*)

Let me end this chapter with something that is very practical. Good literature can be such a powerful influence in our kids' lives. I've listed below some books and movies that are sure to inspire a sense of perseverance and to contribute to a young person's passion and zeal for life.

Depending on your child's age and limitations, you may need to find abridged versions of these stories. You may even find it necessary to familiarize yourself with the literature and to tell the story in your own words, in a way that your child understands.

I'm including a very brief description of each book and movie, but it would be good for you to research especially the movies before exposing your kids to them. For example, *Rocky* is a great story about perseverance, but your daughter or son may not be able to handle the "blood and guts" of it. You know your kids better than anyone. Remember, you are seeking to inspire them to a positive outlook. If something is extremely disturbing to them, they will miss the benefit of it.

If you watch a movie or read a book with your children (or even if they watch or read without you there), have some follow-up questions ready to help bring out the message of the story more vividly. This doesn't need to be elaborate or lengthy. Just ask a couple questions such as "What was your favorite part of the story?" "Did you learn anything about perseverance from the characters in the story?" Kids can even learn what not to do and not to be from the bad examples in literature. But they need your help to sort it all out in their minds and to make it as profitable to them as it can be.

Many of the books listed are also available as movies and visa-versa.

SUGGESTED BOOKS
(beginning with books for younger children and moving on to books for older kids)

Little Toot by Hardie Gramatky
Little Toot is a mischievous tugboat who gets himself into trouble and brings shame to his father. In the end, he shows bravery and determination and makes his father proud of him.

The Little Engine that Could by Watty Piper
A train becomes in need of an engine to pull it over a high mountain. Larger engines are asked to pull the train, but refuse for various reasons. But the little engine takes on the task and encourages itself by repeating, "I think I can..." The little engine's determination is successful.

The Treasure Tree by Gary Smalley and John Trent
Four best friends (a lion, otter, golden retriever, and beaver) go on a treasure hunt. Each animal must use the strengths of his own personality in the quest and must also learn to respect the attributes of the others.

Brave Irene by William Steig
Irene is a dressmaker's daughter. Her mother has made a dress for the duch-

ess but cannot get it to her because of a fierce snowstorm. Irene is a girl of "where there's a will, there's a way." She overcomes dangers and wicked wind to complete her mission to deliver the dress.

The Perseverance of Christopher Columbus by Lori Jordan Rice

A fun and educational way to inspire stick-to-itiveness and to look at a real-life positive role model.

Leo the Late Bloomer by Robert Kraus

Leo's dad is concerned when Leo isn't reading, writing, drawing, or even speaking. But his mother knows that Leo will do these things when he is ready. Encouragement for other "late bloomers."

The Carrot Seed by Ruth Kraus and Crockett Johnson

A little boy plants a seed and everyone around him insists that "it won't come up." He continues to work toward his belief that it will come up. And it does. Great lesson on going for what you believe in, in the midst of opposition.

The Gigantic Little Hero by Matt Whitlock

The story of an ant who feels he can't do the job; but his friends help and encourage him and he discovers the secret of perseverance.

Black Beauty by Anna Sewell

The story is told from the perspective of a horse, Black Beauty, who suffers abuse and neglect. It is the horse's determination and courage that sustain him. He finally is led to a loving, good home. The author, Anna Sewell, was in an accident in her late teens and could not walk upright, but could ride her horse.

The Tortoise and the Hare, **a fable by Aesop**

A turtle is ridiculed for his slow ways by a hare. The tortoise challenges his mocker to a race. The hare feels he is so far superior and so far ahead that he takes a nap, but the tortoise keeps going "slow and steady" and wins the race.

The Crooked Colt **by C.W. Anderson**

The little colt is small and his legs are wobbly and crooked. No one pays attention to him except the little girl who believes that one day he will be strong. After a time, he does grow strong, just as his little friend believed that he would.

A Girl Named Helen Keller **by Margo Lundell**

There are, of course, many versions of the life of Helen Keller. This one is a level 3 reader which makes it suitable for young children and good for beginning or struggling readers.

Little Pilgrim's Progress **by Helen Taylor**

A very simple to understand version of the original allegory. There are a number of versions for children as well as dramatizations on CD. The main plot is the perseverance that Christian (or "Little Christian") shows in overcoming all the obstacles to getting to the Celestial City.

Children's Book of Virtues **by William Bennett**

Stories that have been chosen for young people to encourage character traits such as honesty, perseverance, courage, responsibility, loyalty and more.

Children's Book of Heroes **by William Bennett**

True and fictional stories of 'heroes" told to inspire and celebrate character traits such as endurance, sacrifice, and courage.

The Courage of Sarah Noble **by Alice Dalgleish**
Young Sarah Noble and her father travel through the wilderness to build a new home for their family. Her mother had said, "Keep up your courage, Sarah Noble." Although Sarah feels afraid of the dark woods and Indians, she does end up showing courage and learns that to be afraid and yet to be brave is the greatest courage of all.

Little House on the Prairie series **by Laura Ingalls Wilder**
Books are sold in a nine-book set or separately. The perseverance shown by the Ingalls family has long captured the hearts of kids and adults alike. Although the stories are full of adventure and hardships, they have a happy tone and will leave the child feeling good about life. There are also DVD's of the TV series.

Louis Braille/The Boy Who Invented Books for the Blind
by Margaret Davidson
Louis Braille was blinded at age 3. He did well in school due to a great memory, but he wanted to read. He invented the raised dot alphabet still used today throughout the world.

Freedom Train: The Story of Harriet Tubman
by Dorothy Sterling
Harriet Tubman was born a slave and always dreamed of being free. After realizing her dream, she decided to help others become free too by becoming a guide on the Underground Railroad. Her courage and persistence helped more people than she ever imagined was possible.

Endurance **by Alfred Lansing**
The true account of a polar explorer Ernest Shackleton who survived for over a year with his crew on the icy Antarctic seas.

Carry On Mr. Bowditch by Jean Lee Latham

Nat Bowditch had a chance to go to sea. There he discovered that many of the navigational sources used were incorrect and dangerous. He wrote a book *The American Practical Navigator* which is still in use today.

Anne of Green Gables by Lucy Maud Montgomery

Who can describe the perseverance of Anne Shirley? She spends her early childhood as an orphan and just when she thought someone wanted her (Marilla and Matthew Cuthbert), she finds they really wanted a boy and it was all a mistake. She persuades them with honest charm to keep her and she grows up to be a great source of pride and joy to them both. (All ages will enjoy this story. I read an abridged version to my students when I was teaching first grade.)

Oliver Twist by Charles Dickens

Oliver is made an orphan when his mother dies. He endures much bad and unfair treatment during his many adventures in life. It is finally revealed that Oliver's father was wealthy, and Oliver ends up having a good life. The villains of the story come to an unhappy end. It is Oliver's spirit of never give up that keeps him going.

Uncle Tom's Cabin by Harriet Beecher Stowe

A summary of the book might be best for young or sensitive children. But its story is one of determination in the midst of unbelievable suffering and mistreatment. It reveals the heartache and fear that many of the slaves endured, never being able to settle into a peaceful life situation because for fear of being sold to an even worse situation. The good character demonstrated by the slaves, especially Tom, humbles those who have been so hard-hearted.

The Chronicles of Narnia by C.S. Lewis

My husband's favorite character in the "Chronicles" is Puddleglum, a

Marsh-wiggle. He has a true heart of great courage, as demonstrated in *The Silver Chair* and *The Last Battle*. There are many characters to observe and admire for their persistence and other character qualities. Some are more "human" than others, such as Edmund who is easy to tempt to wrong-doing in *The Lion, the Witch and the Wardrobe*. But Lewis shines forth the theme of sacrifice and redemption when Aslan the great lion dies in Edmund's place and redeems him.

Joni by Joni Eareckson Tada

Joni's first book which tells of how her diving accident as a teenager caused her to be paralyzed from the neck down. She shares of the awful process of her times in the hospital and of her depression and hopelessness. The true story ends triumphantly as Joni comes to realize the love God has for her and of the hope that her life could be made into something wonderful for God's glory and the encouragement of others.

The Hiding Place by Corrie Ten Boom

I mentioned earlier in this book that my family had listened to a dramatization by Focus on the Family of this story. That is a very good choice for young people because although it expresses the suffering involved during Hitler's reign and extermination of millions of Jewish people, it also brings out some of the humor and the lighter times of the Ten Boom family to balance out the grave experience that they had. Still, the child who hears this story will leave with an awareness of the potential evil that exists in the human heart; yet, they will be more impressed with the reality that Betsy Ten Boom expressed with her dying breath—that no pit is deeper than God and His love can reach.

MOVIES
(Beginning with movies for the young)

Ice Age
Determination begins the movie with Scrat holding tightly to his beloved acorn and refusing to let go no matter what. Later, a group of prehistoric animals are determined to return a lost baby to his tribe. Wholesome humor with some good character demonstrated.

Chicken Run
The Tweedys run a chicken farm somewhat resembling a World War II POW camp. Perseverance is demonstrated as the chickens are determined to be free. "It's not the fences around the farm that keep us here. It's the fences around your brains."

Adventures from the Book of Virtues
Animated television series showing forth the same character traits as the anthology of stories contained in William Bennett's book.

October Sky
Homer Hickam is a kid with a bleak future—to work in the coal mines. When Sputnik goes into orbit, he becomes inspired to build rockets. He and his friend seek to do just that through trial and error and are ridiculed for it. One teacher understands and helps them with their determined efforts, letting them know that they could be contenders for prizes in the national science fair—college scholarships.

Inn of Sixth Happiness
The true story of Gladys Aylward who must gather a large group of orphaned children and lead them across a tormenting trek over mountains and through

obstacles of various kinds. The adventures bring out the strong, determined, yet gentle character of the woman who cared enough to try to do what should have been impossible.

Radio

Based on a true story of a mentally challenged young black man who always carried around a radio. He shows interest in the high school football team and the coach gives him a chance to be a part of it. The townspeople don't like this, but Radio wins their affection and confidence over time. To this day, he works with the football team at that high school.

Iron Will

When Will Stoneman's dad dies, he decides to enter a dog-sled race in order to save his family from losing the farm and financial ruin. He uses his father's best dog Gus at the head of the dog team. But he finds that fighting the elements (and doing that is brutal!) is only half of his challenge. Dealing with the greedy and egotistical co-racers is the other half! It makes a person cold and tired just watching this movie, but it is inspirational to keeping one's eyes on the goal.

Apollo 13

Everyone thought that the Apollo 13 was just another routine space flight in 1970, but due to some mishaps, the crew ended up being stranded 205,000 miles from earth. With resources, such as oxygen, running out, the crew engaged in a desperate battle to survive. The theme of the movie is summarized in the line, "Houston, we have a problem."

Chariots of Fire

True story of Eric Liddle, an Olympic runner. His greatest test of perseverance comes when he has to stand by his convictions to not participate on Sunday because of his faith. He does make that difficult decision, even though running is so important to him. In the end, he gets to run a different race that is not on Sunday. He then goes on to be a missionary, which is where his heart had always been.

Rudy

A story about having enough persistence and determination to try to reach your dreams no matter what the odds. Based on a true story about a boy who wanted to play on the Notre Dame football team. Rough language.

I hope that this list of literature will be of help to your family. Happy reading, watching, and discussing!

YOUNG PERSEVERANCE

Ending this chapter is a poem about "never give up" written by a young person who realizes the significance of perseverance:

I will never give up
No matter what the odds are
No matter what people say
No matter how far
I will never give up

Even when it seems all over
Even when no one else believes
Even when it seems I can go no further
I will never give up

For I know I have strength within
For I know I can persevere
For I know that I can win
I will never give up

Because it's someone else's fault
Because I am settling for good enough
Because I fear that I will fall short
I will never give up

There is so much I can still do
There is too much talent to waste
There is so much in me that I want you to see
I will never give up

If I do, I will not be the best me that could live
If I do, I will never know what I am capable of
If I do, I am not giving the world all I can give
I will never give up

—Written by K.D., Age 15 —Oregon

CHAPTER SIX

Group Study and Discussion Questions

1. Read Proverbs 24:16. Why is this kind of perseverance especially important for the child who has challenges that are difficult?

2. Review the section "The Goal: Less Support." How can parents and special kids "get stuck" in having the parent do more for the child than is necessary? Summarize in your own words what "scaffolding" is and how it applies to parenting a special child.

3. How does thinking long-term motivate you as a parent to encourage your child to do things that are difficult for him or her?

4. Can you think of an example where your child is able to say, "I can't do that, but I *can* do this"?

5. Review the section "Rebound! What To Do With Failure." Why is the concept of being able to "rebound" after failure so freeing? Can you share an example of when you or someone in your family was able to rebound and start over?

6. How do you think that having a positive outlook can help a special child to persevere when life gets tough? Were there any items on the list of 10 suggestions to turn the focus toward positive things that you would like to try? Can you add any of your own?

7. Read Psalm 127:1-2. How can you apply this truth of God's ability to areas that you feel stressed and tired in right now?

8. Have you seen in your life or your child's life that good literature can be uplifting? Share some specific literature (in the form of books or movies) that has encouraged you.

Encouraging Physical Health

Beloved, I pray that in all respects you may prosper and be in good health, just as your soul prospers. (3 John verse 2)

It may seem rather disjointed to end a book with a chapter on physical health when the themes have been focusing on inward qualities. But it is really not disjointed at all. I know firsthand that if the physical body is ill, and specifically if it is ill with allergies and sensitivities to food and the environment, it is difficult to even function, let alone to develop a growing sense of character.

Earlier I mentioned that I had developed a condition that seemed to be autoimmune in nature and resulted in symptoms much like the symptoms that autistic children experience—intolerance of food and environmental factors; a crushing, buzzing sensation from "reactions" that affected me from my head all the way down to my toes—and every part in between; a sensitivity to lights, sounds, and smells. I was only able to eat a few foods that did not send me anywhere from a mild to a severe reaction, and because of this, I weighed 96 pounds. I'll tell you, I feel for kids who might experience these kinds of responses to their environment—it's like being allergic to your own planet! As an adult, I sometimes felt I was going crazy, and hate to think of what it would feel like to a child.

During the time that I was confined to one room because of my illness, I did a lot of studying, and it was the results of gathering and applying this information that, coupled with God's healing grace, I was able to get well to the point that I can function normally, and in many ways, am healthier than ever before.

I could easily write a book on what I learned, but if I were to summarize it in one sentence, it would be: *Intestinal health is everything!* Our "gut" or intestine is the center of our overall health. Here is what Jordan Rubin has to say about how important the intestine is even to our emotional well-being:

Fully one-half of your nerve cells are located in the gut, so your capacity for feeling and for emotional expression depends primarily on the gut (and only to a lesser extent on your brain). By the time you add together the number of nerve cells in the esophagus, stomach, and small and large intestines, there are more nerve cells in the overall digestive system than there are in the peripheral nervous system.

Most people would say the brain determines whether you are happy or sad, but they have their facts skewed. It seems the gut is more responsible than we ever imagined for mental well-being and how we feel.[1]

As Mr. Rubin points out, there's more to the phrase "gut feeling" than we may realize!

This means that antibiotics should be reserved for only very serious situations. Avoid running to the doctor for antibiotics every time your kid gets a runny nose. The term "anti" means "against" and "bio" means "life." Those antibiotics that are so effective in killing bad bacteria also wipe out the "good bacteria" in our intestinal track; the importance of these "good guys" cannot be overstated! We need to continually feed and replenish the "probiotics" in our intestines ("pro" meaning "in favor of" or "for," thus probiotic meaning "for life"). There are diets and lifestyles that contribute to good intestinal health. I'll be sharing a few things that have been most helpful to my family and me. May what I learned be of some help to you.

KID'S HEALTH ISSUES

Kids in recent times have different health issues than in the previous generation or so. Child diabetes, obesity, and allergies have escalated in the last couple of decades. For the special-needs child, the condition that is most prevalent of these is allergies. The reason? Allergies are brought on in part by a compromised immune system, and kids who have weaknesses of various kinds are more vulnerable to an immune system malfunction.

The kinds of severe reactions that occur more and more often go beyond the old idea of "hay fever"—runny nose, itchy eyes, and sneezing. The reactions can be debilitating. Autistic children often have these kinds of allergies. The proverbial question of "which came first the chicken or the egg?" arises when observing that so many of these autistic kids have allergies. Did the allergies contribute to the condition of autism or did the autism bring on the allergies? I certainly have no decisive answer to that question, but will offer that when autism is considered to be "an incurable brain disorder," there is little hope of seeing much improvement. If, however, there are some environmental and nutritional factors, there is a chance of bringing about a change in the condition. A parent can't go wrong to approach the problem by improving the child's health and seeking to pinpoint the exact sources of sensitivities. There is nothing to lose and everything to gain when doing everything you can to strengthen your child's immune system and to help lighten the load of environmental and food reactions.

Autistic children are not the only kids who suffer from allergy problems. Any child with special issues will be more prone to allergies and environmental sensitivities because they tend to have more surgeries, take more antibiotics, are prescribed more medications, and in general have more opportunity to weaken the immune system.

SO, WHAT'S A PARENT TO DO??

The good news is that no matter what health challenges your child may face, the basic answer to the question, "What's a parent to do?" is really the same, for good health habits will positively affect any person and does not need to be greatly individualized.

The following are some basic health principles that can help everyone in your family gain more vibrant health.

DIET

You probably have heard the phrase, "you are what you eat." Although the organic hippy movement of the 60's laid hold of this phrase, those who quoted it first came much earlier. In the 1800's Ludwig Andreas Feuerbach wrote: "Der Mensch ist, was er ißt." That translates into English, as "man is what he eats."

In a purely physical sense, nothing could be truer. Of the factors that are in our control (and granted, there are some that are not in our control), diet will affect our health, either for good or for bad, more than anything else.

Fats.

A low-fat diet for children is usually a bad idea. They need good fat in their diet to grow and to develop properly. Elizabeth Walling gives this explanation:

> Children need a diet higher in fat compared to adults. They need around
> 5-10% more calories from fat than adults do. This is because, even though
> children are smaller in size, their bodies use an enormous amount of energy
> in support of growth and development. This includes the development of
> nervous system, immune system, bone structure, and muscle tissue.[2]

It's not an issue of how much fat, but rather what kind of fat that we need to concern ourselves with.

You likely have heard that "hydrogenated" oils are not good for you. But you may not know exactly why. Read the following description by Sally Fallon concerning what hydrogenated fats really are:

> Hydrogenation: This is the process that turns polyunsaturates,
> normally liquid at room temperature, into fats that are solid at
> room temperature—margarine and shortening. To produce them,
> manufacturers begin with the cheapest oils—soy, corn, cottonseed or
> canola, already rancid from the extraction process—and mix them
> with tiny metal particles—usually nickel oxide. This oil with its
> nickel catalyst is then subjected to hydrogen gas in a high-pressure,

high-temperature reactor. Next, soap-like emulsifiers and starch are
squeezed into the mixture to give it a better consistency; the oil is
yet again subjected to high temperatures when it is steam-cleaned.
This removes its unpleasant odor. Margarine's natural color, an
unappetizing grey, is removed with bleach. Dyes and strong flavors
must be added to make it resemble butter. Finally the mixture is
compressed and packaged in blocks or tubs and sold as health food.[3]

Needless to say, after reading that, we should avoid putting that stuff into our kids' bodies as much as possible!

I like to feed my family butter, olive oil, and coconut oil. I know you've probably heard bad tales of butter and of tropical oils like coconut oil, but these are actually good oils and will benefit the body.[4]

Sugar.

A friend of mine used to call sugar "granulated iniquity." Unfortunately, white sugar really is pretty evil when it comes to health. But that doesn't mean we can't ever satisfy our kids' sweet tooth. God has actually given us a guideline in the Scriptures about sweets:

My son, eat honey for it is good. (Proverbs 24:13)

So far, so good! But then there is the restriction:

It is not good to eat much honey. (Proverbs 25:27)

So, the two verses in combination say that God has provided sweet things such as honey to enjoy, then hastens to add, but not too much!

How much is "too much"? That varies with the individual. My 85-year-old mom seems to be able to eat sugar without restriction with no negative effect! But my paternal grandma, my dad, and my brother all died from complications from diabetes, so it's nothing to mess with. Some can tolerate a little more, and some a little less, but we all should be careful.

Refined sugar is something to be avoided, but honey is actually good for us in small amounts. Here's what Jordan Rubin, author of *The Maker's Diet* writes about honey:

> *The creator chose to use honey to describe the abundance of the Promised Land; calling it the land of "milk and honey." (Exod. 13:5) Honey is one of the most powerful healing foods we have at our disposal. Generations of grandmothers prepared hot honey drinks to soothe sore throats, calm frayed nerves, and ensure a good night's sleep. Asthmatics often swear by honey's ability to help them breathe easier. Honey wipes out bacteria that cause diarrhea. And honey may eliminate such disease-causing bacteria as salmonella, shigella, E. coli, and cholera.*[5]

So be creative and make some tasty treats with honey or pure maple syrup. There will be some recipes later in this chapter.

Grains.

Many kids, especially those who have special issues, cannot tolerate wheat and in some cases, gluten. I said earlier that trying to bestow good health upon our children need not be terribly individualized, for applying the same health principles can be good for just about any health problem. However, when it comes to avoiding certain foods because of allergies and sensitivities, it becomes a very individualized matter. It often takes some detective work to identify what is making our kids not feel well. I can't tolerate wheat but I can eat spelt, which contains gluten. Some people can't eat this, others can't eat that. It seems that everyone is unique in his or her sensitivities and often there appears to be neither rhyme nor reason to the whole thing. I can eat chocolate but I can't tolerate green beans...go figure! Trial and error is the best method of discovering hidden food allergies.

I would offer a suggestion that could help your children who are sensitive to grains come to a place where their bodies stop seeing these grains as an enemy: Sprouted grains are far easier to digest because the process of sprouting (or germination) neutralizes enzyme inhibitors. Or to say it more simply, germination of grains aids in the digestive process and the body is less likely to "take offense," or to view the grains as an unwanted invader. Of course, if your child has very severe reactions to grains, it might not be a good idea to experiment even with sprouted grains.

To make sprouted-grain bread is reserved for the talented in culinary arts! But there are some easy ways to get sprouted grains into the diet. Alvarado Street Bakery makes delicious sprouted bread and can be found in health-food stores as well as in some regular grocery stores. It is also possible to soak grains and seeds to make porridge. Simply doing this brings your grains "to life" as it releases enzymes and increases the retention of vitamins and minerals. Look for the recipe "Super Enzyme, Slow-Cooking Porridge" at the end of this chapter.

Rotating grains is a good idea even if there are not any sensitivities— yet. One reason that so many people are allergic to grains such as wheat and corn is because we have overeaten certain foods in our culture. If we eat some spelt, kamut, and other grains, our bodies will be less likely to reject any one grain. As Sally Fallon points out, "A (final) cause of food allergies is the present-day tendency to eat exclusively foods from just a few types of families."[6]

Eating grains is a delightful experience; think of warm or toasted bread with butter — nothing like it. But we have to be careful to eat "good" grains, or our bodies may rebel. Start with whole grains (as opposed to refined) and "graduate" your family to sprouted grains. Some families begin with bread that is half whole grain and half white, and gradually work into whole grains and then sprouted whole grains. Old habits die hard, but don't give up on helping your family change their eating habits. It's been absolutely amazing—since our family began eating differently, our illnesses have decreased by about 95%! Some have called whole foods "God's medicine," and I believe it. Eating the right kinds of grains is the best place to begin the change for good.

Milk, It Does A Body Good…but it's not that simple…

Milk sugar (lactose) and milk protein (casein) cause a lot of people, and more and more children, to have allergic reactions or at the very least, an upset stomach. But there is a way to get the nutritional benefits of dairy products and to greatly reduce the likelihood that the body won't be able to tolerate them—that is, to consume only fermented milk products. Fermentation breaks down the casein found in milk, which is a very difficult protein to digest. It also creates enzymes, which greatly help to digest the milk sugar, lactose.

I was surprised to find a couple years ago that although I can't drink a glass of milk without a bad reaction, I can easily consume kefir. Apparently, the fermentation and enzymes have done their job and that leaves my weakened digestive system free to derive only the benefits of the kefir.

Kefir can be made from scratch or you can buy a good brand such as Helios. The store-bought variety comes in plain and flavored. The flavored has a lot of sugar, so I usually mix half and half. It takes a pretty brave soul (a child might especially have a hard time with it) to drink the very sour plain kefir. But it really is delicious with just a bit of "help" and a great way to have milk "do a body good."

The Perils of the American Diet

To conclude this section on food: Just this week I received the following e-mail from our friend Steve, who with his wife Melinda, is doing some missionary/humanitarian work in Uganda. He struggles with multiple sclerosis. He has just returned back to Africa after a couple of months furlough in the United States. Here is what he wrote:

I have noticed a solid immediate connection between my symptoms and MSG. So why do my symptoms reduce in Uganda but increase in the USA? Because MSG and it's various derivatives are often present in processed foods. Processed foods are common in the USA but not in Uganda

Steve had sent this note as a group e-mail and following is one of the replies he received from a friend:

well I never told you my story, I had been experiencing crazy stomach pain on the side of my stomach here in the U.S. before going to Africa, then when I went to Africa the pain stopped I had no trouble eating food there. As soon as I got back the pain came back too...Hmmm funny how only in America we have all these crazy problems but not in other countries?

"Hmmm..." is right!

KIDS WERE MADE TO MOVE!

The body was made to move, especially young bodies—and I mean more than just the wrist and fingers that are required to run computers and video games. Here are just a few benefits of regular exercise for kids:

1. Increases energy. You may be saying, "No thanks! My kid has too much energy!" Well, let me hasten to add that after exercise, there tends to be a relaxed and focused energy, as opposed to "out of control" energy.

2. There are "feel good" hormones called endorphins that are released during exercise. These can temper such things as depression, anger, and anxiety.

3. Enhances sleep. Does your child have sleep problems? I would offer two suggestions: First, limit "random" naps during the day and have a regular sleep schedule. Second, make sure he or she gets to run outside with little structure—just old fashioned "out of breath" play times. Sleep will come easier to the child who gets fresh air and exercise.

4. Exercise is fun for kids! Let them squeal, run, and laugh. Have the band-aides handy. A few scraped knees won't hurt them.

5. Enhances all bodily functions—mental focus, digestion, immune function, circulation, heart, and nervous system, just to name a few!

If there is a physical disability, don't abandon the idea of exercise. When my son was in a wheelchair, we didn't get him a motorized chair so that at least his upper body could exercise and he could have the satisfaction of propelling himself to where he wanted to go. While this may not always be practical or even possible, I do encourage you to think in terms of your child getting as much exercise as possible, even if a therapist has to move his limbs around for him.

There is no lack of information and encouragement from an abundance of sources to engage in a healthy diet and exercise, but sometimes we can hear too much of a good thing and get immune to the message. Try to hear the message afresh and give your children this gift of health.

RECIPES AND "TIPS"

Following are some tips and recipes (both for food and for chemical-free toiletries) that you may find helpful in the quest to make your home a healthier place to be.

Tricks to get your kids to eat healthy food

No matter what your kids' challenges are, they will benefit beyond measure by eating what I call "God's food," that is, the food that God has made to literally be health-giving and healing with every bite—food that hasn't been messed up by processing or adding non-food ingredients.

I read an article recently that said kids will eat more M&M's and with more gusto if the candy is multicolored rather than all one color. Ah ha! A principle to borrow and use for healthy eating: Instead of serving carrots or sliced green bell peppers, serve red, yellow, orange and green peppers with carrots. And try curling the carrots with a special tool found at a kitchen store. Make those raw veggies a tantalizing delight to the eyes, and watch them disappear!

Fruit can be especially fun, making kabobs and smoothies, or simply arranging different colors and shapes on a dish.

Toss the Pop Tarts for breakfast and try making old-fashioned oats too interesting to resist. Swirl pure maple syrup on it; dot it with raisins; put your kids' favorite fruit on it, maybe bananas.

For dinner all you really need to remember (except for allergy considerations) is to make real food, from scratch. Say good-bye to the boxed stuff—too many "mystery" ingredients. Then take your real food and make it as colorful and tempting as possible.

I like to make whole grain bread and with some of the dough make cinnamon rolls using honey instead of sugar (also melted butter, lots of cinnamon, and maybe raisins or nuts) Then let the house fill with the aroma of those warm rolls, and your kids will be devouring whole grains before your eyes. Spelt or kamut can be used in place of wheat flour.

The "trick" is to make healthy food look and taste more appealing than the stale potato chips in the cupboard. It's not hard to do because God has already made the fascinating colors, shapes, and flavors. Just combine them in a way that your children can't resist.

This all takes a little extra time in the kitchen. But ask yourself, would I rather spend time in the kitchen or in the doctor's office? Most of us would choose the kitchen, wouldn't we?!

Recipes for kids with food allergies

In the following recipes there may be some ingredients that need to be modified according to the particular limitations of your kids. But each recipe contains "whole" food as opposed to processed food, and I believe that the body and the immune system crave these whole, real foods in the form that God intended for them to be eaten. Simply eating real food will make for a healthier situation, and the body will be less inclined to develop wrong responses.

Most of these recipes are not gluten free. If your child seems to reject all foods containing gluten, Pamela's Products offer gluten-free and yummy breads and desserts. (www.pamelasproducts.com)

Here are some of my favorite recipes:

This first recipe was found as a result of our home school cultural geography class in which we studied a country and then found a recipe that originated in that country. This recipe is from Brazil. All I can say to describe it is—"YUM!" (Feel free to remove any ingredient that may not fit into your family's diet.)

Brazilian Beef Creole

½ cup olive oil
1 pound flat iron steak, thinly sliced
4 medium potatoes, sliced
4 medium tomatoes, sliced
1 large onion, sliced
1 large green bell pepper, chopped
2 tablespoons fresh parsley and/or cilantro, chopped
2 cloves of garlic chopped (or garlic powder)
salt and pepper to taste
seasonings such as chili powder to taste
1 cup beef or chicken stock
(optional: chopped chilis or hot peppers)

In a large (preferably iron) skillet, heat oil and layer beef, potatoes, tomatoes, onions, peppers, and seasonings. Add stock and a little olive oil over top. Heat medium-high uncovered for 10 minutes. Reduce heat to medium/medium-low and simmer *loosely covered* until potatoes are tender. Serve as is or over rice.

Healthy Banana Bread

3 bananas, mashed
(for the holidays, one cup pumpkin can be used)
2 eggs
½ cup oil (expeller-pressed canola or real melted butter)
¾ cup honey or pure maple syrup
2 cups whole spelt flour
(freshly ground if you have a grain grinder)
1 tseaspoon baking soda
1 tseaspoon baking powder
½ teaspoon salt
1 teaspoon vanilla
optional ingredients: cinnamon, chopped nuts

Mix wet and dry ingredients in separate bowls and then combine. I like to use mini loaf pans, but bigger loaf pans and even muffin pans can be used. Prepare pans with your favorite non-stick method. Bake at 375 degrees for 25 minutes (more for big loaf, less for muffins).

Wheat-Free, Real-Food Casserole

Usually, the bad thing about casseroles is that foods are used which contain a lot of artificial ingredients and preservatives, such as canned cream soups. Here is a casserole made from scratch that contains only "real" food!

In medium saucepan, combine one cube real butter and a handful of chopped onion, carrots, celery, green or red pepper, or any other crunchy veggies you like. Sauté these veggies in the butter until tender.

Add two cups chicken broth (use a brand like 365 from Whole Foods) combined with enough spelt flour to thicken, about ¼ cup. Use a whisk to remove any lumps, then add to the veggie brew in the pan. Bring to a gentle boil, and then simmer until casserole base thickens. Add ½ tsp. salt and some pepper and any other spices that you enjoy such as garlic powder or parsley.

Place this all into a casserole dish and add any (not all) of the following ingredients to make your customized casserole:

Broccoli
Rice pasta
Instant or cooked rice
Chicken or turkey
Mixed frozen vegetables
Cheese (obviously skip the cheese if there are dairy sensitivities)
Or anything else you find in your refrigerator that does not
violate the particular food allergies in your home

Bake at 350 for about 25 minutes or until bubbly.

Super Enzyme, Slow-Cooking Porridge

Soaking brings out vitamins and minerals, and releases enzymes for easy digestion. How nice to wake up to steaming porridge—ready to go!

1 cup old fashioned rolled oats
1 cup oat bran
pinch of salt
6 cups filtered water
cinnamon to taste
2 tablespoons coconut oil or butter
honey or pure maple syrup to taste
raisins

At about 6:00 p.m. combine oats, oat bran, salt, cinnamon, and water. Let sit until bedtime, then turn crock pot on the lowest setting ("warm," if you have that setting).

In the morning, add coconut oil or butter, honey or maple syrup, and raisins, if desired. Use a wire whisk to remove any lumps. If consistency is too thick, add rice milk.

Optional: You may experiment with adding seeds, nuts, and other grains and alternative grains (such as quinoa, millet, amaranth) during the soaking time.

Bev's Immune-Building, Detox Soup

This recipe is meant to be kid-friendly, so I went easy on the intensity. You can boost the medicinal qualities by increasing the amount of all ingredients except the chicken, stock, and salt. You can also add chopped green cabbage.

The soup can be made from scratch—in which case brown chicken and onion before slow cooking all ingredients, including 6-8 cups of water. Or, use 32 oz. ready-made stock (a healthy brand) and about 2 cups water; then add cooked chicken along with other ingredients.

6-8 cups chicken stock

½ chicken (for less greasy soup, remove all or almost all skin)

1 small onion, chopped

½ cup carrots, sliced

½ cup celery sliced

2 tablespoons chopped fresh garlic

1 tablespoon fresh chopped Italian parsley

1 tablespoon fresh chopped kale

1 tablespoon fresh chopped cilantro

½ inch chopped ginger root

1 teaspoon oregano

1 teaspoon ground chili pepper (optional)

1 teaspoon ground cumin

1 teaspoon paprika

salt and pepper to taste

Be sure to slow-cook for maximum vitamin retention. Cook about 8 hours. When soup is finished, add noodles or rice. Add water as needed during cooking time according to your taste.

Gluten-Free Apple Almond Muffins

2 1/2 cups ground almonds or almond flour

1/4 cup unsweetened applesauce

1 tablespoons orange zest

1/2 cup honey

1/2 teaspoon baking soda

1/8 teaspoon salt

2 eggs

Mix flour, eggs, and honey. Add remaining ingredients. Bake at 350 degrees for about 20 minutes.

Crunchy Granola Munchies

Delete or add any ingredients that meet your dietary needs. Be creative with the basic recipe.

⅓ cup honey
½ stick butter
3 cups old-fashioned oats
1 cup chopped nuts including pecans and walnuts
¼ cup sunflower seeds
½ cup raisins

Heat oven to 325 degrees. Combine honey and butter in small saucepan. Heat on low until melted. Combine oats and other dry ingredients in bowl. Pour honey butter over oats mixture and stir well. Spread granola evenly in a thin layer on a baking sheet. Bake for ten minutes and stir. Then bake 10 more minutes. Stir in raisins or other dried fruit at this time. Cool and then transfer to airtight container. Happy eating!

RECIPES FOR KIDS WITH CHEMICAL SENSITIVITIES

These aren't food recipes. They are recipes for things that we put on our bodies like cream and lip balm. The kind we buy at the store contains fragrance and lots of other "stuff" that can be irritating to kids who have chemical and environmental sensitivities.

Because we are "whole" people, lightening your child's physical load can do wonders to help him gain control of other areas of his life. It's quite a burden to have to constantly fight off reactions to things that make you feel bad.

So here are just a few of my favorite recipes. All of these ingredients can be found at a store like Whole Foods.

Skin-Healing Cream *(great for psoriasis, eczema, and very dry skin)*

2 oz. shea butter
1 oz. jojoba oil
½ oz. aloe vera gel

optional: 3-4 drops of lemon essential oil (Warning: citrus oil can cause a reaction in direct sunlight, so experiment before using large amounts)

Stir until blended. You may need to heat a bit to blend. This cream is extremely healing to skin (especially if you add a little vitamin E oil). Use at night or blot off the excess oil with a tissue during the day.

Lemon Hair Spray

I know your kids probably don't use hairspray, but they can react to what *you* wear. This will give your tresses a lemony fragrance and your sensitive child won't be bothered. It holds pretty well too!

Chop up one whole lemon into about eight pieces. Boil in 2 cups water. Simmer about 10 minutes, adding water, if necessary, to replace excess evaporation. You should end up with about 1 1/2 cups "hairspray." Let sit in pan for another 5 minutes after removing from heat. Then pour through a sieve into a measuring cup until cool enough to transfer to a spray bottle. Best to refrigerate between uses. Spray lightly so as not to wet hair. Repeat.

Peppermint Lip Balm

You will need a medium saucepan with about one inch of water in the bottom. Place a small Pyrex measuring cup in the water. Your ingredients will go in the measuring cup, which acts as a double boiler.

Have ready about 4 plastic pill containers, found in the camping section of a store like REI. The smaller the container the better, for freshness. The ones I use are about ¼ inch high.

*3 heaping teaspoons shredded beeswax (You may use a cheese grater
to shred it. Wash the grater in the bottom rack of dishwasher,
perhaps a couple of times, to get clean.)
2 teaspoons jojoba oil (Jojoba is great because it is the closet thing to
your natural skin oils of any oil that exists)
3 level teaspoons shea butter
A few drops of vitamin E oil*

Heat all these ingredients in the measuring cup. After water in pan boils for a while, stir. The ingredients should turn clear. At that point, remove from heat and add:

*4-6 drops peppermint essential oil
Optional for girls: a dab of natural lipstick to tint*

Pour into the little containers. Leave the lid off until set.

Yogurt Face Wash

*8 oz. plain yogurt
3 tablespoons aloe vera gel
3 drops lemon oil* (avoid contact with eyes if using the lemon oil)

Stir and refrigerate between uses. Makes skin feel smooth and soft. Also may be used as a hair conditioner.

GOOD NEWS

There is little we can do to change the environment "out there," that is, outside of our home; but there is plenty we can do to control the environment within our own walls—and especially what we put on our bodies. The good news is that if we successfully make our homes a place where our weary immune systems can get a much-needed break, then we will be more likely to be able to handle what we might have to face when we step outside of our doors. This means that if your child is struggling with sensitivities, there is something very practical you can do that does not involve loading him down with drugs (which often creates problems of its own).

If you are like me, as a parent of kids who have needs that feel beyond what we can control, it's comforting to know that there are some things we can do for them that will really help their situation. Helping them to have maximum physical health is one of those things that we can work on that will really show definite and substantial improvement. It can even be a fun endeavor if we put our minds on a positive track about it. And we are sure to enjoy the benefits such as fewer illnesses and an overall more robust outlook on life that is bound to be the result of improving health.

Group Study and Discussion Questions

1. Read 3 John verse 2. Why do you think the apostle John felt that giving a blessing that involved physical health was important? Comment on how your child's physical health can affect other areas of his or her life.

2. Considering the statement, "you are what you eat," as it relates to physical health, what are some ways you would like to improve the diet of your family?

3. Read Proverbs 24:13 and 25:27. What principles can you glean from these verses about 1.) how God has made food for us to enjoy. 2.) the wisdom of moderation in eating?

4. Review the section "Kids Were Made to Move!" Think specifically of your child's challenges. How do you think regular exercise/physical playtime might benefit him or her? Can you share some good ways that you have found to get exercise into the daily schedule?

5. This chapter shares some "tricks" to get kids to eat healthy food. Do you have any tricks or tips that have worked well for you in feeding your family?

Conclusion

To close this book, I thought you might like to hear from two men in my life—my husband and my younger son.

Let's start with Mike, who has been the best father to our children that I could imagine. As he will share, being the kind of dad that he is did not come instantly but has been a journey for him, learning from his mistakes and growing into the parent that God wants him to be. (Isn't parenting a journey for all of us?) I'll let him tell you about it in his own words...

REFLECTIONS OF A DAD
...BY MIKE LINDER

I Should Have Gotten Smarter Faster

While on a date with my wife recently, she asked me "What would you have done differently in your parenting; and what do you think you have done well?" That question led to the following thoughts.

In answer to the first question of what I would have done differently—I would have gotten smarter faster. Not sure how you do that, but a missed opportunity in my parenting was driven home to me by what transpired with my daughter. I have a clear memory of just the two of us going together to return the rental truck we had used to move to Illinois. The drop off place was in a town over an hour away so we had plenty of time to relate, towing the car and driving across the countryside. On the way back we stopped to eat at Dairy Queen, a top-tier restaurant for a 3 year old, making it an outing to remember. Later I would come to realize this was our first and only outing of just the two of us. All of my daughter Kristie's life I had been working 6 days a week and holidays, too busy to get away much with my family, focused more on my career. I had just left that job to make my home more of a priority, but it came too late for my first child—because a few weeks later Kristie became sick, slipped into a coma, and five weeks later, passed away.

Since then I have worked hard to keep my job from overrunning my home life. I suppose there are times when that limited what I could do to advance my career but I have realized that the two boys, one with physical challenges, who God gave me are part of my mission in life and that takes some time. You can't do everything you would like to do. Most moms have a heart to give their all to their kid's but without Dad's help it becomes more than one person can handle. So the principle for us dads is to see the raising of our children, including the one who might take much more time and effort, as a part of our investment in eternity as followers of Jesus. We have to accept some limits in what we would like to do. I thrive on chasing the mission of the business I am part of but I also have another mission to chase that is equally, if not more, an investment in eternity—the stewardship of being a present father as well as the extra challenge of leading my son with special needs to be all he was uniquely created to be.

Another missed opportunity that I would have done differently is to have helped my older son, Ricky, to know how his sacrifices could really help our family. The sibling of a child with special challenges spends a lot of time doing things like waiting in doctor's offices. Also, there can be restrictions on activities, like in our house where bedtime was earlier and some events were skipped to help minimize common illnesses since they were potentially life threatening to Ricky's sibling. I realized too late that I just required the sacrifices rather than spending one on one time including Ricky in the planning and helping him to "own" the ideas for how we could serve each other in the family. Parents get tired in the struggle to survive and it gets too easy just to tell the kid what to do. I would be more intentional about helping my son come to grips with the whole situation and dialoging with him about his concerns and frustrations. Ricky and Brad have always loved and enjoyed each other, and for that I'm grateful. But more could have been done in the area of communication from me as the dad.

Sledding, Hardy Boys, and Dates With My Wife
(some things I have done right)

Where I work, we evaluate the projects that we have done, reviewing the mistakes we don't want to repeat. That has value. But what I really find most valuable is when we look at what we did right so that we can incorporate those things into future projects.

In the last section, I shared some of the mistakes I have made as a dad. In this one, I want to do the more fun part of sharing a few things I have done right.

I have tried to give our son Brad every opportunity to experience life. As a rule, if we went sledding, Brad went sledding. If we went camping, Brad went camping. If he wanted to go to camp with the youth group, I tried to make it happen. This takes a good bit of extra effort, but the joy has come in seeing my son, who has such hard challenges, blossom into an incredibly fine young man who loves people, loves life, and isn't afraid to tackle a challenge. The apostle Paul told some of his disciples, "You are my joy and my crown." I feel that way about my son.

Even though I could have had more direct communication with my older son, we did spend hours upon hours reading in an overstuffed chair in the evenings, and I read him every kind of book imaginable, from biographies, to classics, to so many *Hardy Boys* books it seems like Frank and Joe were part of the family. Our family was limited in many ways, not being able to travel and to have some kinds of adventures. But Ricky and I had adventures of every kind sitting in that big chair reading. I'm so glad that we had that time together.

One final thing I would do again is that I tried to pull my wife away from her mothering each week to be my special date. We have always gone out together, making the effort to get the babysitter or whatever was needed, so that we could have time for just the two of us. It gave us a chance to remember why we fell in love and married each other and enjoy some time as a couple. I've communicated to the kids that we are a family, but a special subset of that family is my wife and I. I let them know our relationship requires some time for just the two of us. I believe it has been good for them to have tangible evidence that Mom and Dad want to be together.

So those are the thoughts that came out of that question over dinner of what I would change and what I would do the same in my parenting. I wonder what is going to get asked over dinner next week?

A YOUNG MAN'S PERSPECTIVE ON HOPE

Samuel Johnson said, "We love to expect, and when expectation is either disappointed or gratified, we want to be again expecting." A positive and joyful heart is one that is expectant. For the Christian, even though there are plenty of disappointments, the hope we have is real and we have every reason to be expectant.

Following is an essay that Brad wrote when he was going to school in, believe it or not, Latin class! I helped him with a little of the wording, but the thoughts are completely his and reflect the hope that is in his heart.

Sorry the picture he describes isn't included. Black and white just didn't do it justice!

Hope…by Brad Linder
The character trait that I chose is hope (or "SPES" in Latin). I drew a sunrise (east coast) because having hope gives anticipation toward a new day. I wanted to add a lot of color because color is such a hopeful thing. The colors are usually bright and hopeful in a sunrise. It is like the old things from the past are gone, and the sunrise is announcing that there are new, good things to look forward to.

One thing that I hope for in the future is being a better person and a better influence on others. I would like to be encouraging to people, and if I am full of hope, I will be. I think that a hopeful person is a positive person. I think some day I will be a better walker as another part of my hope for the future.

Hope is very meaningful to me because it makes me optimistic and reminds me of my relationship with Christ, who is my salvation. I also admire this quality in other people because it tells me that they have true expectations for the future and purpose in their life right now.

My life would improve if I applied hope to whatever hardships I face; it would make me worry less. Hope can help me to press on when I am in a stressful situation. Hope can be like sunshine when sad or bad things happen. There is always hope no matter what happens.

When I see a sunrise in the morning, it reminds me that each day is new and gives me hope that there will be good things to come.

*Mike and Brad
Linder*

*Ricky and Brad
Linder*

You're Special

"There are no ordinary people. You have never talked to a mere mortal," wrote C. S. Lewis. It's true—each one of us is a special creation of God.

Believe it or not—no one else is just like you. Your physical appearance, your voice and personality traits—your habits, intelligence, personal tastes—all these make you one of a kind. Even your fingerprints distinguish you from every other human being—past, present, or future. You are not the product of some cosmic assembly line; you are unique.

But the most important facet of your identity is that God created you in His own image (Genesis 1:27). He made you so you could share in His creation, could love and laugh and know Him person to person. You are special indeed!

The Bible reveals God's total interest in you as an individual. The psalmist wrote in one of his most beautiful prayers, "I will praise Thee; for I am fearfully and wonderfully made" (Psalm 139:14). God knew you even before you were born. Then, and now, He has plans just for you, plans conceived in love.

As we appreciate God's constant concern for us, we really begin to grasp the awfulness of sin. He loves you and me so much; yet how often we go our own way, turning our backs on Him. God's designs for our lives are then blocked; His mercies do not come to the unwilling.

But even here we are precious to God, for He continues to love us even when we pay Him no mind. He still sees us as individuals with great value. No wonder the psalmist declared, "How precious are Thy thoughts unto me, O God! How great is the sum of them! If I should count them, they are more in number than the sand" (Psalm 139:17,18). God is not an unfeeling, cold-hearted monarch of the heavens. He feels our pains; He shares our sorrows. He cares, and He considers each one of us important enough to love.

In fact, He loves us so much that He gave His only Son to die for our sins. "Herein is love," the Bible says, "not that we loved God, but that He loved us, and sent His Son to be the propitiation [full payment] for our sins" (1 John 4:10).

Because you and I are special to God, He wants to forgive us and give us a full, meaningful life. When we trust in Jesus Christ and let Him put our lives together, the Bible says that we become "God's masterpieces, created in Christ Jesus" (Ephesians 2:10, paraphrase). Can anyone be more special than that?

Yes, you are valuable to God! If you have never trusted Jesus Christ for your salvation, you can pray something like this today:

Lord, thank You for sending Jesus Christ to die for my sins and rise from the dead so that I can know Your forgiveness and live with you forever. Right now I ask Him to be my Savior so that I can live as the special creation that You intended me to be.

—Ted Griffin

Copyright 1982 by Good News Publishers. Used by permission. For more information, visit www.goodnewstracts.org

How To Facilitate a Small Group

Moms/parents who have kids with special challenges can often feel isolated. Having a weekly time to discuss issues that affect us all can be an encouraging and strengthening time for everyone involved.

HOW TO GET STARTED:

Get the word out any way you can think of that a group is starting for moms/parents of kids that have unique challenges (you might stay away from the term "special needs" as some parents whose kids do indeed have needs that are special, shy away from that term, seeing it as a label). Some ways to gather group participants are: put an announcement in church bulletins; invitations by mail (I prefer "snail mail" as many people disregard the excessive e-mails they may receive); and friends inviting friends on an individual level.

Once you have a group of moms/parents who are interested in beginning a weekly time together, it's time to really start planning how it will all work. The following are some guidelines:

1. My suggestion is not to limit the group to parents of kids who have a certain type of issue. This book was designed to address parents of kids who have all different kinds of challenges, and from mild to severe. It's true that a child who has CP has very different daily issues than the one who has primarily physical limitations, for example. Still, you broaden your potential for a wider support base when

you expand the definition of the group.

2. Challenge group members to make a seven-week commitment to study this book. It's very discouraging to prepare a lesson, get refreshments ready, and to put together all that is involved in a time like this, only to have one person show up! Ask the participants to pray about their decision to be in the group and to make it a priority in their week. If they decide to be involved, you'll still have some absentee issues, but at least lay a good foundation by encouraging commitment from the beginning.

3. Give responsibility to each group member. Often there is more commitment to a group when each member is responsible for more than just showing up. Ideas for involvement are: rotating discussion group leaders (among those who are so inclined); bringing refreshments; and making phone calls or writing notes during the week to group members. Try to give everyone a "job." It will make them feel more like a vital part of things.

4. The questions at the end of each chapter of this book can probably keep a group engaged for the full discussion time (I suggest about 45 minutes discussion and 30 minutes or so for casual fellowship.) The leader can also write supplemental questions. Avoid allowing any one person to share too profusely! Encourage the quieter members to share by asking them direct, non-threatening questions ("Megan, do you have any thoughts on…?")

5. Do not allow the discussion to become negative. Although we want to encourage openness about the group member's feelings (and this sometimes means sharing some negative feelings), we also want the time together to be uplifting. If participants share some things that are a burden to them, say, "Thank you so much for sharing. Could we all pray for you about that?" And then do pray—either right then, or at the end of the discussion time.

6. Avoid "bunny trails." A good leader will strike a balance between sticking to the lesson plan and allowing spontaneous thoughts to be discussed. Keep the spontaneous discussions short. Stay as much as possible in the bounds of the discussion questions, knowing that

most of the time, the group member's life issues will be addressed at some point by the planned lesson.

7. Always end in prayer. Many times concerns will come up that seem to have no human answer. Seek God on these things. Most people really appreciate having their needs and concerns prayed for by caring friends.

8. End on time! Give a definite ending time and stick to it. Group members will feel more inclined to attend the group if they know what to expect in terms of leaving time.

9. Do little things to keep in touch between meetings. Be creative. We live in an isolated society, "special moms/parents" can especially feel this loneliness. Do little things for each other to encourage a sense of community among you.

Notes

Chapter 1: *Never Give up on Having Joy*
1. Amy Charmichael, *Rose From Brier* (Christian Literature Crusade, 1980)

Chapter 2: *Never Give Up Showing Unconditional Love*
1. <http://www.autismspeaks.org/family/index.php#tips>
2. Sibling Support Program, http://www.siblingsupport.org/connect/in-sibs-own-words

Chapter 3: *Never Give Up Providing Boundaries*
1. Helen Keller, *The Story of my Life* (New York: Bantam Dell, reissue 2005), 6.
2. Ibid., 9.
3. Richard Louv, *Last Child in the Woods: Saving Our Children From Nature-Deficit Disorder* (New York: Algonquin Books of Chapel Hill, 2008), 102.

Chapter 4: *Never Give Up in Hard Times*
1. Elmer L. Towns, *Praying the Psalms: To Touch God and Be Touched by Him* (Shippensburg, PA: Destiny Image Publishers, Inc, 2004), 26- 246 (Selected Psalms)
2. Ibid., 163.

Chapter 5: *Encouraging Character*
1. Helen Keller, *The Story of my Life* (New York: Bantam Dell, 2005), 23.
2. The Autism News, http://www.theautismnews.com/tag/kyle-forbes/

Chapter 6:   *Encouraging Perseverance*

1.   John Faherty, "Children of Autism Approach Adult World," The Arizona Republic, July 12, 2009. http://www.azcentral.com/news/articles/2009/07/12/20090712autism0712.html

2.   Elizabeth Landau, "Prom King with Down Syndrome Goes to College," CNNHealth, Sept. 30, 2008. http://www.cnn.com/2008/Health/conditions/09/30/adult.down.syndrome

3.   Emerson Eggriches, *Love and Respect: The Love She Most Desires/ The Respect He Desperately Needs* (Nashville, Tennessee: Thomas Nelson, 2004), 106-107.

Chapter 7:   *Encouraging Physical Health*

1.   Jordan Rubin, *The Maker's Diet.* (Lake Mary, Florida: Siloam A Strang Company, 2004), 51.

2.   Elizabeth Walling, "Just Say No: Low Fat Diets are Not For Children," NaturalNews.com, March 25, 2009. http://www.naturalnews.com/02591-diets-food-health.html

3.   Sally Fallon, *Nourishing Traditions* (Washington DC: New Trends Publishing, Inc., 1994, 2001), 14.

4.   Rubin, 150.

5.   Rubin, 15.

6.   Fallen, 57.

To order copies of this book:

go to www.special-heart.com

OR

to contact the author:

bev@special-heart.com